Undoing Yourself Too

Some Other Titles from Falcon Press

Christopher S. Hyatt, Ph.D.
Undoing Yourself with Energized Meditation and Other Devices
Techniques for Undoing Yourself (audios)
Radical Undoing: Complete Course for Undoing Yourself (videos & audios)
Energized Hypnosis (book, videos & audios)
To Lie Is Human: Not Getting Caught Is Divine
Secrets of Western Tantra: The Sexuality of the Middle Path
Hard Zen, Soft Heart

Christopher S. Hyatt, Ph.D. with contributions by
Wm. S. Burroughs, Timothy Leary, Robert Anton Wilson et al.
Rebels & Devils: The Psychology of Liberation

Christopher S. Hyatt, Ph.D. & Antero Alli
A Modern Shaman's Guide to a Pregnant Universe

S. Jason Black and Christopher S. Hyatt, Ph.D.
Pacts With the Devil: A Chronicle of Sex, Blasphemy & Liberation
Urban Voodoo: A Beginner's Guide to Afro-Caribbean Magic

Antero Alli
Angel Tech: A Modern Shaman's Guide to Reality Selection
Angel Tech Talk (audio)

Peter J. Carroll
The Chaos Magick Audios
PsyberMagick

Phil Hine
Condensed Chaos: An Introduction to Chaos Magic
Prime Chaos: Adventures in Chaos Magic
The Pseudonomicon

Joseph Lisiewski, Ph.D.
Ceremonial Magic and the Power of Evocation
Kabbalistic Cycles and the Mastery of Life
Kabbalistic Handbook for the Practicing Magician

Israel Regardie
The Complete Golden Dawn System of Magic
What You Should Know About the Golden Dawn
The Golden Dawn Audios
The World of Enochian Magic (audio)

Steven Heller
Monsters & Magical Sticks: There's No Such Thing As Hypnosis?

For up-to-the-minute information on prices and availability, please visit our website at http://originalfalcon.com

Undoing Yourself Too

by
Christopher S. Hyatt, Ph.D.
&
the Falconeers

Antero Alli • Steven Heller
Robert Anton Wilson • Joseph C. Lisiewski
Israel Regardie • Camden Benares
Timothy Leary • Eric Gullichsen
Pope Nick the One • Jim Goldiner

THE *Original* FALCON PRESS
TEMPE, ARIZONA, U.S.A.

International Standard Book Number: 978-1-935150-72-5
ISBN: 978-1-61869-720-2 (mobi)
ISBN: 978-1-61869-721-9 (ePub)
Library of Congress Catalog Card Number: 88-80928

First Edition 1988
Second (revised) Edition 2014
First eBook Edition 2014

Cover by P. Emerson Williams

The paper used in this publication meets the minimum requirements of the American National Standard for Permanence of Paper for Printed Library Materials Z39.48-1984

Address all inquiries to:
The Original Falcon Press
1753 East Broadway Road #101-277
Tempe, AZ 85282 U.S.A.
(or)
PO Box 3540
Silver Springs NV 89429 U.S.A.

website: http://www.originalfalcon.com
email: info@originalfalcon.com

Dedicated to The New Person

"He divines remedies against injuries;
he knows how to turn serious accidents
to his own advantage;
whatever does not kill him
makes him stronger."

Frederich Nietzsche
Ecce Homo

TABLE of CONTENTS

Forward 9

Trance Formations 15
by Antero Alli

Breaking Trance 20
by Steven Heller

How Brain Software Programs Brain Hardware 22
by Robert Anton Wilson

So You Want To Be Someone 36
by Joseph C. Lisiewski

Another Bedtime Story (The New Law) 45

Guilt And Shame 58

A Trance Is No Deeper Than You Are 68

Philosopher's Heaven and Man's Hell 80

Will And Desire 98

Stars Shine Even When It's Cloudy 104

The Final Words Of A Western Master 110
Israel Regardie, Interviewed by C.S. Hyatt

A Mantram For The Muddled Class 150

Culture Is For Bacteria 154

Yuppies: The New Monotheists 159

Only A Monotheist Can 'No' The Future 164

The Tripolar Formula For Success 172

A Cymbal Is Just A Loud Noise (Statistics: The Science of the State) 176

Do You Want To Be Invisible? 186

The Immortality Option 190
by Camden Benares

Twenty-Two Alternatives To Involuntary Death 196
by Timothy Leary & Eric Gullichsen

Thus Spoke The Pope 216
by Pope Nick the One

The Problem With The World 225

One By One 229
by Jim Goldiner

Who Owns The Planet Earth 230
by Christopher S. Hyatt

Frranzzz! 242
by Jim Goldiner

Why Is It? 243
by Jim Goldiner

Rear Admiral Hyatt 244

Zingots & Dirtlings 245

A
HUMAN BEING
DOESN'T
Automatically
BECOME
A
HUMAN BEING
BY
BEING BORN

S/HE
MUST BE
FORMALLY
ACCEPTED.
THIS TAKES
PLACE AFTER
PASSING
CERTAIN
EXAMS

THESE ARE U-FEM MYSTICALLY CALLED "RIGHTS" OF PASSAGE

THOSE
WHO FAIL ARE:

JAILED / KILLED

READ FALCON
BOOKS

BECOME
STREET PEOPLE

—— or ——

WRITE THEIR OWN EXAMS

TRANCE FORMATIONS

Towards UNDOING YOURSELF TOO

by Antero Alli

The enigmatic dance master and philosopher, Georges I. Gurdjieff, delivered many profound messages to those with ears to hear. He often referred to the word "sleep" to describe the current state of humanity, inferring the possibility of "waking" only after having realized one's "dream"...the trance-like state between these two extremes of our spectrum of consciousness. Once we realize the breadth, height and depth of our consciousness, we are ushered into the totality of ourselves and start nudging a terrible truth: we are multidimensional beings who have settled for a lot less. The **trance of dream** is a signal traversing between the sleeping giant within us and its potential awakening. To know we are dreaming, is the first step to truly awakening. To know we are dreaming, is the first step to truly awakening to our spiritual heritage as fully realized human beings. How do we know we are dreaming? How do we know we are **not?!**

The Aboriginal people of Australia have learned to use their minds in very different ways than the rest of the western world. Instead of building complex technologies and communications systems, they engage in **long-distance telepathy** amongst each other. Where we rely on airline networks to fly us around the globe, they visit faraway places via their "dreambodies" through the aetheric web of their "dreamtime." One of their beliefs about dreams is that they are **continuous**. According to their dream cosmology, we are either **dreaming and/or being dreamed.** For instance, when you go to sleep at night you dream of your "dreamself" going through various adventures and interactions in "dreamland." Aboriginal thought suggests that when we wake up in the morning, our previous dreamself has gone to sleep in order **to dream us.** So, the next time you get up in the morning, consider the possibility that you have entered a dream...dreamed up by your dreambody as it sleeps in dreamland.

Trance is the conscious recognition of this quality of "dream" in our so-called "waking state"...the daydream we call "reality." **We are all sleepwalking.** When were aware of it, we experience trance. Any effort to become conscious of this condition as an art of will is **a trance-induction device.** For example, next time you're in the supermarket, bank and/or department store, see how aware you can be of the hypnotic trance of mass cultural hallucination. Then, see if you can be aware of yourself as an autonomous agent amidst the great sleeping vapor without succumbing to its pervasive effects. As another example, enter these same institutions for the opposite purpose of giving into their hypnotic state as completely as possible just to get acquainted. With some practice, you'll learn to detect the characteristics of collective trance...a preliminary exercise for washing your own brain.

Part Too: Disillusionment = Enlightenment

Strewn about the attic floor of our collective psyche are the shattered remnants of broken promises and future dreams delivered to us by the gods of our primitive past. Throughout history, the names by which these gods were known were many: Momendad, Papamama, Dada, Popma, Mommidaddy, but most importantly...it was the eternal impact of their Forms that entranced our souls with the arch—status traditionally reserved for deities. Meanwhile, deep in the sacred heart of this holy hierarchy, there lived and breathed a child untouched by the trance of Form. This was no fault of the child for its in—no-sense knew No Form and as such, could never be Formed. Here is a story of that child who now lives as a seed in the fertile realms of post—history poised to sprout at the drop of a sunrise. It is also a de—programming device to help you regain the use of your own life. In order for it to work, however, you must be willing to be tricked, swindled, hoodwinked and otherwise fleeced and undone. Your wool will be sold to cover the cost of postage and handling.

This is not a method. The words you are reading are lies. They are a conspiracy to keep you asleep. See how they are combined in such a way as to create the illusion of reality in your mind. When enough words like this are arranged in certain patterns, a rhythm is set up to flood your momentary awareness with the shifting qualities of the trance you're already in. Word Trance. It is so simple, it feels true. Written reality. If it's written, it must be true.

Words are drugs. They change your brain. When you get lost, you find a map and then, you find yourself again. Until you lose yourself again and then, you find another map and find another self again. It's easy. One map per self. Does that mean..."no map = no self"? Or is that a game of loss and gain? Have you missed the bus? Here and now's your only chance.

Imagine the spaces between these words containing the secret of life.

Now, picture a world **without pictures.**

If you're really feeling adventurous, watch the *gaps* between your thoughts e x p a n d .
What ? !
What gaps ?

Did you expect your thoughts to be continuous?

Wouldn't it be nice to be able to *make things go away?*

Have you ever lived without a self-image?

Are you now, or have you ever been, a member of the Community Party?

Eldridge Cleaver's beaver cleaver never went unused until he was born again and washed his sins away with New Lemon Pledges. There's only one, too. You deserve a break today...an emergency brake. Emerge and see. Break the trance. Enter the control room. Kill the projectionist. If you're feeling too guilty, just pull the plug. Watch the zen dropcloth. Listen to the squealing pigs in the trough. Breakfast time. Honey, I'm home! Kellogg's best to you. Don't drive drunk. Brake fast. Break trance. (I brakedance for animals.) We have entered a state of emerge and see. We open no mind before it's time when I wish upon a star, it's the real thing in the back of your mind...what you're hoping to find. Today's star is tomorrow's black hole. Ask anyone who's been there. When the Light hits, the Dark gets tough. Gravity sucks. The electrical cock. Polarized lenses keep the sun out. Polarization gets you out of the kitchen...fast...fast...fast relief! Refreshes without filling...

THE MOST OFTEN, OCCASIONALLY & RARELY ASKED QUESTION

1) The most often asked question: *"How are you feeling?"*
2) The occasionally asked question: *"What are you feeling?"*
3) The rarely asked question: *"Are you feeling?"*

Instructions for those who are in over their heads:
When in deep waters become a diver.

Your body is like a diver's suit.
It is now time to check your outfit for leaks so you won't drown in your depths.
Are you deep enough to be shallow?
If not, it's best to stay onshore for this expedition.
If you're shallow enough, take this moment to *fantasize a very shallow sexual experience.*

This exercise has been designed to seduce and repulse you. Inexpensive, subliminal advertising tactics were employed to catch your attention and hold it long enough to plant **seed concepts** for the purpose of future recall and symbolic manipulation. This, in turn, suggests the effect of rewiring your conceptual circuitry for easy-access, remote-control viewing from the master program which you did not originate. To cancel this program, please take a deep breath and turn the page. Simon says, "take a deep breath and turn the page." Turn the page if you're awake.

BREAKING TRANCE

by Steven Heller, Ph.D.

How do you know when you're getting too close to a fire? Of course, by feeling the heat! But what if you were unable to feel the heat? You would probably not know until you were burning yourself or you smelled your flesh burning. So many people go through life in such a deep trance, that they do not know when they are heading for trouble until they have stepped into it. They no longer know what they feel, want or need!

A small child hears his/her parents fighting and becomes afraid. They tell conflicting stories and s/he becomes confused. They send out incongruent messages and the anxiety rises to painful levels. One day s/he discovers that by "dropping out" and going off into inner-space-out, everything is better ... for a while. If I can't feel it, hear it or see it, it can't get me. **TRANCE IS BORN!** Of course, if a truck is coming at you and you respond by "Not seeing or hearing it" I guarantee that you will feel it. Your trance will simply prevent you from getting out of the way.

A child enters a new and exciting world called school. S/he is curious and open to learning. "Children, we must all sit just like this and always raise your hand and there is one right way to do things and of course only one right answer!" says the adult called teacher. Day in and day out s/he sees things but is told they don't really exist. S/he feels things and is told that the feelings are not real and s/he doesn't really know what s/he feels in the first place. The secret of survival? Go into a trance! The result ... years later s/he doesn't feel what there is to feel, can't hear what

there is to hear and can't see what needs to
Frustration, failure and pain is a constant companion.

The secret ... **BREAK TRANCE!** You must learn
question and question some more. You can not trust what you have been tranced into seeing, hearing, or feeling. Tonight, when you go to sleep, sleep on the other side of the bed; sit at a different seat at meal times. For the adventurous, eat with your left hand (or right hand if you are left-handed). Read a book...from the last page to the first page; record conversations with those you have the poorest communication with. Look for problem areas instead of avoiding them and then come up with three of the most unusual methods for solving the problem. Put a rubber band on your wrist and snap it when ever you feel yourself "dropping out."

Learn to talk to those parts of you that know the difference between trance and what is happening around you. For example, imagine that you begin to feel anxiety. Ask your inner guide to change the feeling into a picture: first a picture of what the feeling itself looks like, and then ask that part to change the picture into one that will help you discover what is really happening for (or to) you. Learn to hear the sound of colors and feelings and to see the feelings and sounds. In short, shake up your systems and break your patterns. (For many interesting and provocative methods of breaking trance, you might even purchase my book, *Monsters and Magical Sticks: There's No Such Thing As Hypnosis.*) Last, but not least, find a good hypnotist who will help you to use hypnosis and trance to end your hypnotic trance.

BRAIN SOFTWARE PROGRAMS BRAIN HARDWARE

by Robert Anton Wilson

As everybody with a home computer knows—and everybody who uses a computer at work also knows—the software can change the functioning of the hardware in radical and sometimes startling ways. The First Law of Computers—so ancient that some claim it dates back to the dark Cthulhoid aeons when LBJ and giant reptiles still roamed the Earth—tells us succinctly, "Garbage In, Garbage Out" (or GIGO, for short). The wrong software *guarantees* wrong answers. Alternately, the correct software will "solve" previously intractable problems in ways that appear "miraculous" to the majority of domesticated primates at this primitive stage of evolution.

I propose that the principle software used in the human brain consists of words, metaphors, disguised metaphors and linguistic structures in general. I also propose, and will here try to demonstrate, that the Sapir-Whorf-Korzybski Hypothesis, as it is called in sociology—"A change in language can transform our perception of the cosmos"—becomes intuitively obvious with a simple experiment in altering brain software by changing the structure of our language.

The human brain has been called a "three pound universe" (Hooper), an "enchanted loom" (Sherrington), a "bio-computer" (Lilly), a "hive of anarchy" (Wolfe), an "intellectual intestine" (de Selby), etc., but whatever one calls it, it remains the most powerful data-processor known on this planet. (It has been estimated by Hooper and Teresi that to duplicate all brain functions in a solid-state computer with 1987 state-of-the-art technology would require a machine as tall as the Empire State Building and as broad and long as Texas.) The brain, like your desk computer, does not receive raw data. It receives such data as it has been built to receive, and it processes the data according to the programs (software) that have been put into it.

Consider the following columns of easily-comprehensible sentences and see if you can determine the major structural difference between Column 1 and Column 2 considered as software for the human brain:

Column 1	**Column 2**
The electron is a wave.	The electron appears as a wave when recorded by $instrument_1$.
The electron is a particle.	The electron appears as a particle when recorded by $instrument_2$.
John is lethargic and unhappy.	John appears lethargic and unhappy in the office.
John is full of fun and high spirits.	John appears full of fun and high spirits while on holiday.
The car involved in the hit-and-run accident was a blue Ford.	In memory, I think I recall the car involved in the hit-and-run accident as a blue Ford.
This is a fascist idea.	This seems like a fascist idea to me.
Beethoven was better than Mozart.	I enjoy Beethoven more than Mozart.
This is a sexist movie.	This seems like a sexist movie to me.

The first column consists of statements in ordinary English, as heard in common usage at this superstitious and barbaric stage of Terran evolution. These statements all assume the viewpoint which philosophers call "naive realism"—the belief that something called "reality" exists somewhere "out there," beyond our brains, and can be directly perceived by our brains. Scientists, as well as philosophers, now agree that such "realism" can only be described as "naive", because no two people ever perceive exactly the same "reality," a fact well established in perception psychology, general psychology, sociology, etc. And, in fact, no two animals perceive the same "reality": each species has its own *umwelt,* or reality-tunnel made up of the signals which the senses and brains of that species can apprehend and comprehend. Worse: instruments perceive different "realities" also, as General Relativity and Quantum Mechanics have amply demonstrated.

It has been emphasized by Niels Bohr, P.W. Bridgman, Bertrand Russell, Count Korzybski and others that sentences of the sort found in Column 1 not only "ignore" the experimental relativity of perceptions but also subtly condition our brains to "ignore" or forget this relativity, if we ever learned it, or even to avoid noticing it at all. As Korzybski especially emphasized, these "Aristotelian" sentences act as software tending to program us to assume attitudes of dogmatism, unwarranted certitude and intolerance.[1]

By comparison, the second column consists of parallel statements rewritten in *E-prime,* or English-prime, a lan-

---

[1] Such sentences have been designated "Aristotelian" by Korzybski because they tacitly assume the Aristotelian philosophy, which pictures a world of block-like entities inhabited by ghostly "essences" or "natures" which can be known with certitude by two-valued logical deduction. This seems so normal in our culture that many feel astounded to learn that the typically Oriental philosophy of Buddhism envisions a world of interactive *processes,* not entities; doubts the universal validity of two-valued logic; and claims the world can only be approximately or relatively understood, not known with certitude.

guage based on the work of Korzybski and proposed for scientific usage by such authors as D. David Bourland and E.W. Kellogg III. E-prime contains much the same vocabulary as standard English but has been made isomorphic to quantum physics (and modern science generally) by first abolishing the Aristotelian "is" of identity and then reformulating each statement phenomenologically in terms of signals received and interpreted by a body (or instrument) moving in space-time.

Concretely, "The electron is a wave" employs the Aristotelian "is" of identity and thereby introduces the false-to-experience notion that we can know the indwelling Aristotelian "essence" or "nature" of the electron. "The electron appears as a wave when recorded with instrument$_1$" reformulates the English sentence into English-prime, abolishes the "is" of identity and returns us to an accurate report of what actually transpired in space-time, namely that the electron was constrained by a certain instrument to appear in a certain form of manifestation.

Similarly, "The electron appears as a particle when recorded by instrument$_1$" evades Aristotelian dogmatism and forces us to *operationalize* or *phenomenologize* our report by stating what actually happened in space-time—namely, that the electron was constrained by a different instrument to appear in a different form of manifestation.

Note well (and please *try* to remember) that "The electron is a wave" and "The electron is a particle" create contradiction, and have historically led to debate and sometimes violent quarrel (e.g., "I did not call my learned colleague an ass-hole. I called him a blithering idiot.") At one time these Aristotelian mis-statements (bad software)—attempting to say what an electron "is"—appeared to justify the opinion that parts of physics can only be expressed in terms of almost surrealist paradox—i.e., within the same Aristotelian logical-linguistic structure, many physicists circa 1920–1930 were led to proclaim that "The universe is illogical" or "The universe does not make sense," etc.

On the other hand, as Bohr first noted, the E-prime alternatives—"The electron appears as a wave when constrained by $instrument_1$" and "The electron appears as a particle when constrained by $instrument_2$"—do not appear *contradictory* but *complementary.* They do not lead to debate or violent quarrel they do not portray the world as bizarre or irrational and (not coincidentally) they simply report what actually took place in the space-time of actual experiments.

Although Dr. Bohr did not formulate E-prime—or even Danish-prime, Danish being the language in which he habitually wrote and probably thought—the basis of E-prime can be found in his Principle of Complementarity and the Copenhagen Interpretation of physics which he created in collaboration with his students circa 1926–28.

The American physicist P.W. Bridgman (like Bohr, a Nobel laureate) first generalized the Bohr approach by articulating the specific principle that scientific propositions should be stated in terms of actual *operations.* If we rigorously follow this rule, we will eventually find ourselves writing E-prime if English serves as our normal language—or in French-prime if we regularly write French, etc. We will have exchanged obsolete Aristotelian software for modern scientific software. We will then program our brains differently, formulate different thoughts and (almost certainly) learn different perceptions or styles of perception.

For the benefit of students of philosophy, although both Bohr and Bridgman appear to have been chiefly influenced by the actual (and startling) experiments in 1920s quantum mechanics, their major intellectual influences appear to have been Kierkegaard, in the case of Bohr, and William James, in the case of Bridgman. Thus, the logic of modern physics, and of E-prime, not only serves as an isomorph of the quantum world but also as the natural way to present the key ideas of Existentialism and Pragmatism. As I have already hinted, E-prime also closely resembles the principles of Zen Buddhism and of phenomenological sociology, as influenced by the radical Existentialist Husserl. This suggests that E-prime may not only clarify debates within science but also prove useful in daily life—if we wish to think pragmatically or existentially or in terms of experienced events in space-time rather than thinking metaphysically of "ghosts in the machine," i.e., abstract essences haunting block-like entities.

Already one suspects that a great deal of the misunderstanding of, or total confusion about, certain non-Aristotelian systems derives from the fact that most writers, not habitually using E-prime, have discussed these systems in ordinary English, which introduces Aristotelian structures into non-Aristotelian data and thus breeds chaos and endless paradox. Once again, "Garbage In, Garbage Out." Aristotelian software does not transduce non-Aristotelian data.

As an experiment, any reader who has had problems understanding quantum physics, Zen, Existentialism or phenomenology should try rereading a book on each and translating all sentences with the Aristotelian "is" to new sentences in E-prime. You may then come to share my suspicion that the difficulties are not found in the subjects but in the use of the wrong language to discuss the subjects—the wrong software for the data.

Looking at the next two sentences in Column 1—"John is lethargic and unhappy" and "John is full of fun and high spirits"—we again encounter contradiction, and we may well suspect pathology. The inexperienced psychiatrist, indeed, might quickly pronounce that John "is" suffering from a manic-depressive psychosis. And, of course, others with a less clinical orientation might rush with equal haste to decide that one set of reports must be due to careless observation or downright lies, and accept the opposite reports as totally true. This could lead to lively debate, or actual quarrel about what sort of man John "really is."

(The reader may find it amusing, as I do, that quarrels of this sort—what sort of man John "really is" or what sort of woman Mary "really is"—occur every day in our still-medieval society, even though less than one quarreler in a thousand knows consciously that such debates depend on Aristotelian philosophy and that asking what something "really is" only make sense at all, at all, within the context of Aristotelian definitions of "reality" and "isness.")

The E-prime translations—"John appears lethargic and unhappy in the office" and "John appears full of fun and high spirits on holiday"—do not contradict each other, report the actual observations in space-time accurately, and remind us that we never know or experience John as an Aristotelian essence (a "spook" in Max Stirner's terms) but only as an aspect of a social field, just as we never know an electron as an Aristotelian essence but only as aspect of an instrumental field.

Another linguistic point seems noteworthy here. I absently wrote "on holiday" because I have spent several years in Ireland; and in Ireland, as in England, people do not go "on vacation", they go "on holiday." The choice of metaphors here does not seem accidental. To say that one goes on holiday is to speak the language of the working class, for whom the time off appears merry and playful; but to say one goes on vacation is to speak the language of the ruling class. *Vacation* comes from the same root as *vacant* and reflects what the owner sees when he looks around the floor—a vacancy where John "should" "be". (I suspect that the owner probably thinks some negative thoughts about the Labor Unions and the "damned Liberal" Government that force him to pay John even when John "is vacant.")

I leave it as a puzzle for the reader: Do the Irish and English speak Working Class in this case because they have had several socialist governments, or have they had several socialist governments because they learned to speak the language of the Working Class? And: has the U.S., alone among industrial nations, never had a socialist government because it speaks the Ruling Class language, or does it speak the Ruling Class language because it has never had a socialist government?

Moving along, "The first man stabbed the second man with a knife," although it contains no explicit Aristotelian "is", continues the Aristotelian assumption that the brain directly apprehends and comprehends "objective" "reality". Dropping this monkish medieval software and trying modern scientific software we get the E-prime translation, "The first man appeared to stab the second man with what appeared to me to be a knife." This accurately reports the activity of the brain as an instrument in space-time, evades Aristotelian dogmatism, operationalizes or phenomenologizes our software—and, incidentally, may spare us from the traditional embarrassment of Psychology Students if we happen to land in a class where the instructor inflicts a certain notorious experiment upon us. In the case of that experiment, the first man actually makes stabbing motions, without stabbing or piercing, and with a banana, not a knife.

Most students, in most cases where this experiment has been performed, actually *see* a knife instead of a banana. (Another reason for doubting Aristotelian software: perception and inference mingle so quickly and feed back to each other so totally, that one cannot existentially untangle them.) Together with John-in-the-office and John-on-holiday, this should illustrate vividly that E-prime has applications beyond physics and on into daily life. It should also make clear that the software of Aristotelian structural assumptions in standard English indeed programs the brain to malfunction—"Garbage In, Garbage Out." (Further illustrations of how the brain, running on Aristotelian software, populates the world with hallucinations and projections can be found in my books *Prometheus Rising, Quantum Psychology* and *The New Inquisition*, among others.)

Similarly, "The car involved in the hit-and-run accident was a blue Ford" seems inadequate and obsolete Aristotelian software—as many eye-witnesses have discovered with some pain during skillful cross examination in court. The E-prime translation into modern software, "In memory, I think I recall the car involved in the hit-and-run accident as a blue Ford" would remove a lot of fun from the lives of lawyers but seems more harmonious with what we now know about neurology and perception psychology.

Again, "This is a fascist idea" contains Aristotelian software, unscientifically omits the instrument from the report, and perpetuates dogmatism and intolerance. Translated into post-quantum E-prime software, this becomes "This seems like a fascist idea to me," which scientifically indicates the instrument being used to constrain the data—in this case, the evaluative apparatus of the speaker's brain. Note one more time that "This is a fascist idea" contradicts "This is not a fascist idea" and provokes quarrels (in which each side seems likely to arrive at the conclusion that the other side "are" damned idiots or worse). "This seems like a fascist idea to me" does not contradict "This doesn't seem like a fascist idea to me" and merely registers the fact that the space-time trajectories of two brains, like two Einsteinian instruments, will yield different readings of the same space-time events.

Our next example, "Beethoven is better than Mozart" might bring the difference between Aristotelian and post-quantum software into clearer focus for many. As formulated in standard English, this assertion implies, if analyzed philosophically, that there exist indwelling essences, or "natures," or spooks, in the music of Beethoven and Mozart, and that Beethoven's spooks "really are" better than Mozart's spooks. Since no such spooks are findable in space-time, the debate about this issue, formulated in this software, can go on forever or until somebody gets so bored that he resorts to blunt instruments to silence the debaters.

The translation into E-prime, "I enjoy Beethoven more than Mozart" reports accurately a series of space-time events—enjoyment processes in the brain of the speaker. This does not contradict another speaker's alternative report, "I enjoy Mozart more than Beethoven," and both reports can profitably be classed as complementary in Bohr's sense.

I cannot resist a minor digression. Although I have only read, and never heard, the endless debate between Mozart maniacs and Beethoven buffs, on one occasion I did hear such a Thomist or medieval debate about Bartok. This happened in a restaurant in Dun Laoghaire, Ireland, and the debaters, two *Englishentities* (a word I have coined to avoid the human chauvinism implied in *Englishpersons*) grew increasingly heated and hostile as they argued. The male Englishentity insisted that Bartok's music "really is" rubbish and junk and noise etc. The female Englishentity insisted, *au contraire,* that Bartok's music "really is" wonderfully new and experimental and exciting etc. I found it excruciatingly hard to avoid the temptation to walk over to their table and explain E-prime to them. I think the main reason I resisted the temptation lies in many often-repeated experiences that convinced me that Englishentities recognize an American accent as soon as they hear it and most of them "know", or think they know, that any American—or any other non-Englishentity—"really is" stupid and uncultured compared to any Englishentity, and they therefore simply would not have listened to me. Such Englishentities have developed a remarkable skill in looking simultaneously polite and bored while engaged in not listening to non-Englishentities—as the Irish, the Hindus, the Africans and numerous others have noted before me.

Finally, "This is a sexist movie" contains Aristotelian metaphysics implying indwelling essences or spooks within the film. The E-prime translation, "This appears a sexist movie to me" includes the observer and the instrument (the observer's brain) in the report and programs the brain with modern, rather than medieval, software. And, again, "This is a sexist movie" contradicts "This is not a sexist movie," while "This appears a sexist movie to me" does not contradict but complements "This does not appear a sexist movie to me."

(One is tempted to add that the whole *bon ton* debate about sexism "in" movies appears only an "intellectual" sublimation of the older, cruder debate, surviving in more primitive areas, like Little Rock, Arkansas, or the U.S. Congress, about indwelling "obscenity" "in" movies. E-prime software takes the fanaticism out of such debates, removes Aristotelian metaphysics and places us back in the phenomenological world of how individual brains process their experience in space-time.)

A further illustration of these principles appears *a propos.* Once while speaking before the Irish Science Fiction Association at Trinity College, Dublin, I was asked, "Do you believe in UFOs?" Evading the temptation to launch an oration on the disadvantages of the yes-no logic of "belief" and the advantages of the modern logic of probability and percentages, I answered simply, "Yes." The questioner then grew excited and offered a long argument that UFOs "really are" those rare meteorological events called "sundogs." I replied simply that he appeared to believe in UFOs also. He then grew more excited and denied vigorously that he "believed" in UFOs, even though he had just moments earlier argued that (a) UFOs exist and (b) he knew what all of them "really are."

This story amuses me because I have read a great deal of the literature of the UFO debate and almost all of it seems constrained by Aristotelian software processing the brains of the debaters. So-called "Skeptics" can just as accurately be dubbed "Believers": they merely believe different models than the so-called "Cultists" or heretics. The "Skeptics" believe, very fervently, that "all" UFOs can be identified as "really being" *ordinary* hallucinations, or hoaxes, or sundogs, or heat inversions, or weather balloons, or the planet Venus, etc. The "Cultists" or heretics believe, some as dogmatically as the Skeptics but some (oddly) more tentatively, that "all"—or maybe only some—UFOs can be identified as spaceships, or time-machines, or secret weapons (of the US or Russia or a hypothetical surviving Nazi underground) or *non-ordinary* hallucinations, etc. Among those who have chosen the model of "non-ordinary" hallucinations, Dr. Carl Gustav Jung proposes that UFOs represent an evolutionarily important eruption of new energies from the "collective unconscious," Dr. Jacques Vallee argues that UFOs have been created by brain manipulations of some unscrupulous and unidentified intelligence Agency; and Dr. Robert Persinger suggests that UFOs result from external-world energy fluctuations—leading to weird lights (probably ball lightning), jumping furniture, electrical malfunctions etc.—and also altering brain waves so that internal-world hallucinations occur.

From the point of view of Aristotelian software, the important issue appears that of choosing which of these conflicting models to "believe." From the point of view of post-quantum software, the important issue appears that of not "believing" any model but estimating (as far as possible) which model seems most probable in a given case or set of cases. Post-quantum software would also probably incline us to accept Bohr's Principle of Complementarity and accept different models on different occasions, for different space-time events.

It seems probable that the prevalence of Aristotelian software in most brains at this stage of evolution accounts for the ubiquitous prevalence of dogmatic belief in one or another UFO model among both "Skeptics" and "Cultists"—and also explains the relative rarity of multi-model zeteticism.

A more controversial illustration of brain software in action: in Chicago in the 1960s, I knew a pacifist, Joffrey Stewart, who spent most of his waking hours walking the streets distributing anti-war pamphlets. Some of these broadsides Joffrey had written himself; some had been written by others but seemed worthy of circulation according to Joffrey's standards. However, Joffrey did not distribute anybody's pamphlets without first "correcting" them in accord with his own software or reality-tunnel or system of semantics. Specifically, he would place question marks before and after any word that seemed to him to imply unexamined and nefarious assumptions. The words that bothered Joffrey most seem to have been "our" and "we." If you received a leaflet by, say Noam Chomsky or Dave Dellinger, after it had been revised by Joffrey, you would see sentences like the following (I am paraphrasing from memory, but I believe I capture the spirit of Joffrey's Criticism of Language):

"...and ?our? taxes are being used to napalm infants..."
"...to defend ?our? standard of living..."
"...these atrocities ?we? are committing..."
"...and why, after all, are ?we? in Vietnam?"

It appears that the Aristotelian "is" of identity should not be considered the only glitch in our brain software. Joffrey Stewart's question marks certainly led me to revise my own software, and I cannot listen to TV these days without mentally inserting similar interrogations in many widely used expressions. When I hear Mr. Reagan described as "our President," I think of Joffrey writing this as "?our? President"; and, then, of course, I recall that less than 25 percent of eligible voters elected Mr. Reagan, the other 75+ percent either voting for somebody else or showing their skepticism and/or contempt by not voting at all.

At this point it seems advisable to quote Korzybski: 'I have said what I have said; I have not said what I have not said." For instance, a while back I set a little trap for careless and Ideologically impassioned readers, by pointing out that in a specific context the word "sexism" should only be used in relation to evaluative processes in the brain of the speaker. From this existentialist-phenomenologist (or operationalist) truism, certain readers probably deduced the inaccurate conclusion, "This author denies that anything to be called sexism exists in the objective world at all." Once again, the wrong software caused the signals to go awry.

Nothing in my remarks implied that using the word "sexism" to describe a company that pays female workers wages averaging less than fifty percent of comparable male workers' wages should be related only to the evaluative activities of the brain of the commentator. Quite the contrary. The operationalist approach here would relate the word "sexism" to the economic data demonstrating the measurable existence of the wage differential.

An old example in physics will clarify this. If an iron bar has a measured temperature of 98° Fahrenheit, what would you expect to find in measuring the temperature of an electron in the bar?

If you guess 98° Fahrenheit, you appear to be using the wrong software. If you say that the question cannot be answered without more data, I suspect you still haven't got the right software for this test.

Some books will tell you that "an electron has no temperature." More accurately, I think, one should say that the word "temperature" has scientific meaning at, or above, the molecular level, but has no meaning below the molecular level. Temperature measures the *movement* of molecules and hence cannot be meaningfully applied to sub-molecular processes.

Thus, to say that "sexism" must be considered operationally to refer to evaluations in a brain when speaking of art works does not mean that "sexism" must always refer *only* to such internal matters. When speaking of economic practices, "sexism" has meaning in relation to economic statistics. This parallels the situation in physics, where "temperature" refers to molecular movement in meaningful statements, and loses all meaning when one attempts to apply it to sub-molecular phenomena.

In conclusion, I would like to suggest, again, that these arguments for post-quantum software (language structures) have as much application and practicality outside science as within science. The cutting edge of philosophy—everything that can be called post-Nietzschean—represents a similar struggle against the increasingly obvious malfunctions of Aristotelian categories; one finds this recognized among such seemingly opposed groups as the Cambridge Linguistic Analysts and the Paris Situationists. Modern literature at its liveliest or most inventive—I think of Joyce, Pound, Borges, Faulkner, Beckett, O'Brien, Williams, Burroughs, Ginsberg—represents a series of strategies to break out of the Aristotelian software of our culture by creating non-Aristotelian linguistic grids. Modern painting took on non-Aristotelian traits as early as 1907 and music at about the same time. To the extent that we remain hypnotically entranced by Aristotelian language structures we become isolated not only from science—and, as I have hinted, from such exotic and interesting systems as Buddhism—but also from the lively and innovative part of modern culture generally.

SO YOU WANT TO BE SOMEONE

Adventures In The Polarized Self

by Joseph C. Lisiewski, Ph.D.

So you want to be "someone"! This is the eternal cry of everyone who has, does, and will ever walk the face of this earth. It is the universal panacea which has littered the language of that drone-mass termed "humanity." Its distillate, that Elixir of tangible result, will dissolve the sphere of confusion, pierce the anvil of socially induced chaos, and rend asunder forever that leprous contagion of self-doubt and inability whose forebears were the dust of parental imitation and the dirt of required mimicry. Unfortunately, such emotionally stirring words and images, bandied about by the reigning social poets and philosophers of our time, cannot create that nearly perfect set of conditions which enable *anyone* to become "someone." What are the conditions necessary for such a transformation? This idealized, yet thoroughly workable process is not a startling revelation given here for the first time. As such, it will be a grave disappointment to those occult bookstore haunting freaks who scan the shelves for the secret quick-fix. Rather, it is an intelligent approach: direct in definition, application, and result. It will truly bring about a transformation in the user which, ironically, will be the reason for its mainstream non-use.

The Use of Structure

Everything of permanence possesses structure. From a physical object to a complex idea, all are the embodiment of structure which lends meaning to their essence. So is the process of becoming "someone." To aid visual memory, refer to the diagram below. Notice the sequence of steps, and the interdependence of Blocks 1, 2 and 3 + 5, while Block 4 serves as a foundation for the 5th. Notice carefully the labels and interrelationships, for our discussion rests upon this understanding.

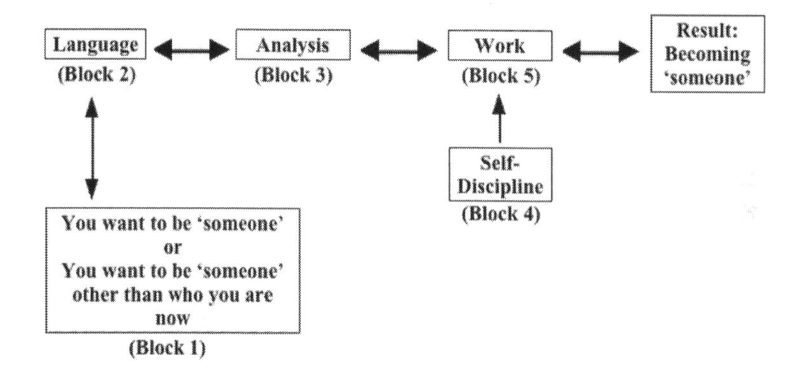

The Structure of Chaos
or
The Path of Transformation

The Elements of Chaos
or of
The Path of Transformation

In the beginning of the quest to be "someone" (Block 1), the seeker immediately encounters the problem of Language (Block 2). The driving emotion to be "someone" is seen as one side of this need, while the concept embodied in the word "someone" is viewed as the other side. This naturally leads to Analysis (Block 3), the next step in the process. These sequence of events constitute a normal rhythm in Self-Discovery: they are part and parcel of the mechanism of human thought to attempt to find, or create, order in chaos.

With analysis, the individual's past is brought into stark focus. Here, an awareness of the constant barrage of thoughts, actions and reactions, goals and desires upon him are made plain. But what is also important is the individual's awareness that these mental occupants of his past possess a strange and elusive quality: they generate a sense of vague, disturbing incompleteness which intensifies as the analysis continues. At the same time, he realizes that what he calls "himself" is the product of their interactions. There is now born deep within the emotional core, a restlessness to discover why and from what point this feeling originates.

With further effort, the now completely restless seeker finds the answer: those irritating feelings; his reactions to the influences of his past and to what he has become as a result of them, are due to his survival instinct. It is not the wanton need for food, sex, or drink; but rather the impetus toward a need for unity of the Self: that Self which up to now was fragmented. What is occurring, metaphorically speaking, is the attraction of all those diffused bits of *personal* thoughts, ideas, and desires to each other, like so many bits of iron filings to a magnet.

Now the attentive reader may say, "Of course I realize all those little bits of what I call my Self want to get together and operate as a well-oiled machine. Everybody knows that!" The problem is that the attentive reader never takes the necessary step which the *tortured* does: that of active involvement in the process. For in the case of the latter, his agony has been self-inflicted by the restlessness brought on through his own deep analysis. He has realized that to be "someone" seems contrary to those not-quite-the-right-fit feelings, thoughts, and ideas which still occupy the corners of his mind, and which lie in direct opposition to his recently activated survival instinct. He has discovered that this instinct is now in the permanent "on" position, and he can never be content with himself as he is. There is only one solution: to continue this investigation in Self-Polarization.

Somewhere in all this literal misery of change, a further insight occurs. Whether it's induced by sleep, a fine meal an inspiring poem, or a chemical tablet matters little; its advent is what counts. It's a phenomenon which has been likened to a psychological break-through, or a little-understood Law of Being, or simply as surrender to the problem. What started out as the use of language to fathom the meaning of being "someone," to give the conscious vocabulary a bull's eye on which to focus, comes back full circle. Specifically, the individual has become aware of the *trance of language.*

The action of this trance has impaired the efforts made so far, but not completely hindered them. The individual now realizes that while in this state, he has used his language of definition to assure himself that he already is "someone," and defined and re-defined himself within his world of belief. Finally, by adhering to his relentless yearning to understand, he sees that the meaning behind the desire to be "someone" really is his desire *to be "someone" other than who he is now!* Instantly, the person's grasp of this fundamental idea leads to the uncovering of the greatest crime ever committed upon any individual or group. It is this trance of language that induced him to become what he is, to feel what he does, and to worship as instructed. In so doing, it produced the sense of incompleteness which caused his search to begin. This crime of the trance language is perpetrated on each and every person from the moment of birth, until the lid of the coffin is sealed. It is used by those who were and are with you all of your life. In the person's early stage of development, he is told to "be the shining apple of his parents' eyes," which was found to really mean: "get good grades in school," but not so good as to surpass Daddy's and Mommy's accomplishments; "don't get a girl in trouble" (or if female, "don't get in trouble!"); "wash behind your ears," showing parental love by your inspection before leaving the house, and "wear clean underwear in case you're hit by a car and taken to the hospital," lest it reflects upon their role as good, decent, caring parents. Gradually, the image of being the "shining apple" of their eyes came to be defined as becoming miniatures of them in thought, word and deed. The young individual has found that he is now liked by his parents because he doesn't offend them, and they receive faint praise from the neighbors whom they secretly hate. So, the need for the security they provide (physical of course, while the youngster's Soul is being raped hourly) is reinforced by his actions which require further abandonment of his innate freedom of thought and expression. By now however, the individual has accepted this. This action-reaction mechanism of behavior progressively spreads outward into all social contacts: mates, friends, job associates, etc., like ripples in a pond. In the end (the point where the person finally decided he wanted to be "someone"), the person finds he is merely the reflection in thought, language and deed of that multi-faceted world we term Society. And the resulting social intercourse we so endearingly hear of simply means, you've been screwed up again!

But our great hope of salvation lies in that permanently switched-on survival instinct spoken of earlier. We now grasp *our own personal* feelings, thoughts and actions which are normal for us. Now is perceived those elements of that genuine, real Self, that "I" deep within. By the process of language awareness and analysis, the true human duality is seen: the hypnotically induced life of society versus the authentic life which comprises Self. The individual has achieved complete polarization.

So far, so good, or so it is thought. But now the person pays the price for his fantastic discovery and decision to become "someone" other than who he was. Throughout the process changes have begun: the old friends somehow seem different. Looking at them gives a curious sense of seeing images in a cracked mirror. They too sense something, and begin to shy away—but only a little at a time, at first. The thing most dreaded becomes more intense: a growing disgust for the values, concepts, and requirements foisted upon the individual during the now dim past of his life. He undertakes a merciless examination of everything: religion, politics, mates, vocation, life, death, meaning, and contradiction. All are in a constant state of analysis by the rapidly becoming "someone." In the latter phases of this transformation, the individual feels as though he were completely isolated from everyone, and void of all substance within. And so it should be, since for all practical purposes those players on his life-stage—those desires and needs, those things to have and to have not that peopled and occupied the world of that former Self—are no longer valid. The sublime, artistically balanced whole they formerly presented are finally seen to rest on a foundation of distorted wants and demands instilled in him by others. The requirements of the demanding new role as "someone" other than who he *was* are now accepted without further pain or refusal. The individual is now ready to implement his new insights and goal needs into his active life-stream.

The infant new "someone" now needs the tools to enable him to manifest the effects of his transformation. In all cases of such change there are at least two driving impulses which characterize the change:

(1) The need to express the new "someone" in terms of reality, i.e., to achieve something which harmonizes those personal thoughts, feelings, and drives. It may be the acquisition of more education to evidence some long hidden vision; it may consist of the honing of some skill, or the development of a talent which not only contributes to his new sense of wholeness, but which is a veritable product of it. Yet again, it may be displayed as a complete change in worldly vocation. All are possibilities.

(2) An earnest yearning to leave behind a creative legacy to future generations. This can be a book, a painting, an idea or concept, a code of behavior others have learned from him, or any of an infinite number of possibilities.

To fulfill these necessities, to manifest them as a genuine result, requires two more activities:

(1) The acquisition and application of self-discipline (Block 4) directed into

(2) Work (Block 5).

This is where many potentially vibrant and vital human possibilities are lost, due to the completely misunderstood nature of self-discipline and work. Again, the individual's negative reactions toward each are the result of society's views of them having been placed into us.

Self-discipline is not a grim process of painful adherence to a technique leading to accomplishment. It is a conscious practice which uses scientifically proven principles that change behavior patterns to enable the new "someone" to do what he requires of himself. Instead of acting from negative behavior, such as avoidance of effort to achieve something, the individual builds into his mint and physical nervous system new positive behavior patterns. Now, he finds himself acting automatically to simulate and exhibit action and reaction patterns which bring with them the successful achievement of his self-imposed visions. It works both ways: just as negative behavior and visions (or mental imaging, if you wish) initiate wrong action or non-action to produce failure, positive behavior and mental images create the corresponding mechanical right action to bring about a favorable result. Self-discipline is a technique and form of conduct which can be very successfully used in any area of life. It is recommended that the serious individual consult the applied psychology section of his library or local professional book shop. Several excellent books and tapes are available on the subject, which will prove to be one of the best investments anyone can make.

Work (Block 5), when engaged in by a self-disciplined person, produces positive results. It is not the feared bug-a-boo taught to you by those beer-guzzling, TV addicts of society who feel work is the curse by which they earn their daily bread. With this attitude, their daily bread is all they earn—and deserve. Rather, work is the purposeful direction of energy toward a goal for the sole purpose of achieving it. It is not to be dreaded, but embraced. It does not merely give life meaning, it is an intrinsic quality of life itself, and the new "someone" has an instinctive feeling this is how it should be. The individual's vistas are now opened and clear. He has changed, and through the use of self-discipline and work, has made the effort necessary to integrate the results, which were created by this process, a real-world experience. He is barred from nothing—most of all, by himself.

Epilogue

This chapter may be viewed by many readers to be radical in nature and content. This has been done on purpose, since the great number of such writings is too often presented in a simple, stale, soothing manner meant to placate the crippled mentality of a dull world. Such is also the purpose and intent of Dr. Christopher S. Hyatt, the author of the highly acclaimed *Undoing Yourself With Energized Meditation* and many other books. Dr. Hyatt has established a daring new approach in the exposition of those psychological and philosophical topics which are of such serious interest and need in the world today. He has turned the tables as it were, on the so-called sophisticated approach in *writing to educate.* Instead of a bland, piecemeal style, he employs rebellious style and attitude in disclosing scientifically valid, psychologically sound principles aimed at bringing about change within the reader: positive, useful, fruitful change. Through this approach he has ruthlessly exposed the fake sense of respectability of the functionally unconscious mass of humanity. In so doing, he has shocked them in making them aware that their so-called respectability lies in the shadow of their pseudo self-dignity. Hyatt has actively *applied* the instruction of the late Alchemist, Frater Albertus, to "shock people out of their insensibilities so they may wake from their sleep, and bring about a world of their *own* design."

TAKE A BREAK

_ _ _ _ _ _

WAKING UP

NOW

Another Bedtime Story

The future of history was altered on March 15, 1923, when a scheduled outing of the Morane family was delayed due to the fact that Mrs. Morane was unexpectedly suffering from her monthlies.

The family was preparing to leave for a camping trip in the woods of NW California, when Mrs. Morane suddenly experienced her period. Due to the fact that the cabin did not have inside plumbing, the trip was delayed for five days. During that time two men had escaped from a maximum security prison, and when the Morane family arrived they were held hostage for 15 days, during which time Mrs. Morane was repeatedly raped by one of the convicts.

A month later Mrs. Morane missed her period and it was assumed that she was pregnant. As an orthodox catholic Mrs. Morane could not consider abortion. Thus she and her husband had the child.

Late in December of 1923 they delivered an eight pound boy.

The scene moves to the year 1993. Mrs. Morane's son is now the President of the United States and is preparing to sign a new law which will have drastic consequences for the planet earth.

A little history might be in order here. In 1988 the pope arrived in the United States and announced that every catholic who uses any form of birth control was automatically excommunicated. You can imagine the hysteria which broke out at the time. Pleas were made to the current president to talk to the pope about his decision.

The President refused to intervene and the 1988 election was believed to have been heavily influenced by the pope's behavior. American catholics, being very concerned, established Vatican West in the State of New York and elected their own pope, who of course was pro-birth-control, and anti-abortion.

In 1988 a conservative was predicted to be a shoe-in, but because of the president's refusal to intervene a leftist-hot-shot-libertarian-adulterer was elected.

During his reign the country experienced rampant inflation, as well as a re-birth of secular individualism. Art prospered, science grew by leaps and bounds, the old industries were re-born into high-tech co-operatives, new forms of education evolved, experimental brain-change drugs and electronic devices were encouraged, space travel flourished, all money being spent on Star Wars was rechanneled to immortality research, the Ayatollah moved to Beverly Hills and became a Rock and Roll star, "work" was renamed "fun," *Undoing Yourself* became the number one best seller for 52 weeks straight, *The 12th Planet* became household reading, *Angel Tech* became a kindergarten classic, *The Game of Life* was used as a model for creative and experimental doctoral dissertations at Harvard, Dr. Heller's *Monsters and Magical Sticks* was used for the de-hypnotization of terminal adulthood, Dr. Donald Holmes author of the *Sapiens System* became the head of the American chapter of the Illuminati Conspiracy, Robert Anton Wilson headed up the Resurrect Wilhelm Reich Fund, Sasha Greenleaf Westerly, author of *Extraterrestrial Growth and Expansion* became the interior landscaper for the newest space lab, taxation was replaced by a lottery (Christopher Hyatt, Ph.D., director), the boredom of sham Sunday services was replaced by spontaneous religious experiences, California therapists were no longer required to turn in members of esoteric groups (such as the Golden Dawn and the OTO) as *prima facie* child abusers, the bible was renamed *Classic Cosmic Comics* which was read weekly on the White House steps by Camden Benares (author of *Zen Without Zen Masters*) to entertain historians and householders and the religion departments of all reputable universities were transferred to the Archeology Department (Artifacts Section). (No doctorate degrees were awarded as this study was considered non-productive.) The earlier attempts to convert religion to psychology were nipped in the bud by the appointment of Thomas Szasz as Secretary of Sanity who converted all mental institutions to sewage treatment plants and by the transfer of pre-scientific psychologies (such as those of Freud and Jung) to the History Department. All shrinks were given honorary degrees in Medieval Studies. Statues in honor of George Gurdjieff, Aleister Crowley, and Israel Regardie were erected in Beverly Hills, California.

Not everything was perfect yet. Inflation was still a problem, but Dr. Leary's experiments to replace fiat money with data were very promising. This was a tremendous threat to the olde pope who had no more dogma to sell. By peddling all the golden idols of rabbi jesus and the saints, and by subsidizing a book entitled *The Sex Life of the Catholic Gods* (Falcon Press, 1988), he raised enough flatulent money to begin a counter movement led by our hero Joe Morane the bastard son of a sodomized tight ass bitch and a criminally insane father.

Thus, not so behind the scenes a backlash was brewing which was to have serious consequences in the election of 1992. Joe's platform was a return to the good olde days, of good ole boys, beer stained t-shirts, old fascism child abuse (discipline), nuclear war families, child and female servitude. Women were segregated into two categories: good (mothers, daughters and wives) and bad (dykes, sluts and bimbos). (Bimbos, as we all know, are the women who hang around boats and sailors.) He promised the return of the factory, the gas guzzler, the draft, the cafeteria, non-alcoholic Sundays, segregation of minorities, no inter-breeding, imprisonment for fornication, the death penalty for drug use, mandatory prison sentences for other victimless crimes, the regulation of the press, censorship of all Falcon Press titles (except, of course, *The Sex Life of the Catholic Gods*), regular sex, strip mining, HARD work, a removal of the ban on "defense" spending, non-birth-control, no abortions, removal of all non-orthodox non-christian churches from our soil, a new religious psychology, and "treatment" camps for AIDS related people.

His motto was Buy American/Marry American—Save the Gene Pool. Father knows best—free use of Group Think facilities—Breed early/Breed often. Fight for American purity. American blood was never wasted. Return to the dollared economy. Jesus was our Founding Father and the First Real American.

In other words, everything was to return to normal, as it was in 1987.

Morane was elected through the pope's money who finally sold his wardrobe to come up with the extra cash, and by the stuffing of the ballot box. The motto was "vote early and vote often" and the ex-mayor of chicago headed the campaign. At the victory celebration party (men and bimbos only) there was much illicit drinking and celebration. All the upstairs rooms were guarded by the secret service to prevent any leaking of sex scandals that the opposition party was sure to make up. The leaders of the born-again movement, resurrected and redressed in tuxedos were crying, speaking in tongues, and falling into spontaneous daily emissions.

After things settled down President Joe, now nicknamed Baby Doc, gave his acceptance speech on black/white TV. His first new law was to make plastic surgery illegal. He felt this contributed to the downfall of the nuclear war family. However, the main event was yet to follow; a few days later the secret law which was to affect the entire planet was to be announced and immediately signed.

TO BE CONTINUED IN UNDOING THREE

JUST KIDDING OF COURSE

SOFTEN UP
— RELAX —
Eyes hard to the Right
No's to the Left

This NEW LAW (as with all others)
Defines the Parameters of the

$$\frac{\text{MASTER}}{\text{SLAVE}} = \text{RELATIONSHIP}$$

MASTER - SLAVE = NON-MASTER?

MASTER + SLAVE = ?

MASTER - SLAVE = REGULAR PERSON?

M × S = ?

MASTER - SLAVE = REGULAR HUMAN ?

M – S = NON-MASTER?

These Definitions are ALWAYS A QUESTION OF OWNERSHIP

POLY

TICS

WHO OWNS THIS FINITE BEING ?

The NEW LAW
is

SIN TAX

SYN TAX

SIN TAX

SYN TAX

SIN TAX

SYN TAX

SIN TAX

SYN TAX

SIN TAX

SYN TAX

SIN TAX

TAX

SYN

and the

price is

GUILT AND SHAME

Heroes

& Humans

do not require

Guilt & Shame

to know what

to

DO!

The Eyes Have It!

UN DOING YOUR SELF TOO

— Some of us feel guilty for choices we have made —
— Others feel guilty for choices they did not make —
— Still others feel guilty for acting without choices —

GUILT EXISTS IN TWO CATEGORIES:

GUILT IS A DIFFICULT TOPIC

It is muddled IDEOLOGIES—few of us are free—fictions poured into our brains as children create emergency flight/fight reactions which have no relationship to the existential world.

Psycho-neurological reactions unceasing collective rituals blinded to the integrity of true human beings fighting for hir right to influence his world.

MORAL FIBER
FOR THE RELIEF OF CONSTIPATION

For those with a caste iron stomach.

For those with a whim of molten steel.

For those who are always right.

For those who are morally superior.

TRY
MORAL BRAN
A NUTRITIOUS FLAKE
(SUGAR COATED OR PLAIN)

I have been asked the following question by someone with lots of MORAL FIBER.

How do we KNOW what's RIGHT and what's WRONG?

Morality is a Word of Those in POWER who accuse rebels of Miss-spelling (Falling out of Trance)

●

It is accompanied by

FEAR — — —

TREMBLING — — —

and

LOOSE

BOWELS — — —

Once found GUILTY

hang your head in

SHAME

and

REPENT

●

UNDOING YOURSELF TOO

ARE YOU

AWAKE?

YES ☐ NO ☐

The major non-violent method of controlling people is SHAME. Now we address this most powerful and terrifying issue.

SHAME SHAME SHAME SHAME SHAME SHAME

SHAME SHAME SHAME SHAME SHAME

SHAME SHAME SHAME SHAME

SHAME SHAME SHAME

SHAME SHAME

SHAME

SHAME SHAME

SHAME SHAME SHAME

SHAME SHAME SHAME SHAME

SHAME SHAME SHAME SHAME SHAME

SHAME SHAME SHAME SHAME SHAME SHAME

DO NOT BE H-Y-P-N-O-T-I-Z-E-D BY SHAME

STAY AWAKE N O W!

SHAME SHH AME SHH AIM SHE AIM

"She Aims Her Bow And The Arrow Silently Strikes The Heart Of Her Victim."

It is believed that Shame is Feminine while Guilt is Masculine.

It is also believed that like these two forms of control, there are two forms of HYPNOSIS. One is called Mother Hypnosis and the other Father Hypnosis.

Each form of hypnosis creates trance through different means, and the effects have similarities and differences. Mother Hypnosis is soft, subtle and shame-based. Father Hypnosis is gruff, guilt-based and direct. Father says "Go to sleep or else"; Mother says "Darling, don't you think it's time to go to sleep?"

Which form of hypnosis is the easiest to UNDO?

(A) Father Hypnosis

(B) Mother Hypnosis

Which form has affected you the most?

(A) Father Hypnosis

(B) Mother Hypnosis

A TRANCE IS NO DEEPER THAN YOU ARE

A TRANCE IS NO DEEPER THAN YOU ARE

A TRANCE IS NO DEEPER THAN YOU ARE

A TRANCE IS NO DEEPER THAN YOU ARE

A TRANCE IS NO DEEPER THAN YOU ARE

A TRANCE IS NO DEEPER THAN YOU ARE

A TRANCE IS NO DEEPER THAN YOU ARE

A TRANCE IS NO DEEPER THAN YOU ARE

A TRANCE IS NO DEEPER THAN YOU ARE

A TRANCE IS NO DEEPER THAN YOU ARE

A TRANCE IS NO DEEPER THAN YOU ARE

A TRANCE IS NO DEEPER THAN YOU ARE

A TRANCE IS NO DEEPER THAN YOU ARE

A TRANCE IS NO DEEPER THAN YOU ARE

STOP NOW

Be clear in your TRANCE -- navigate:

0 — — — — — — — — — — — 100%

As you have begun to see, your tense-shun is related to lumping things together which you would prefer to separate. Let it go NOW! Separate! Let the pieces go.

PILOT TO NAVIGATOR

Stand erect - NO SHAME -- LET IT GO -- Forgive the Earth -- The World is Not Your Fault.

NAVIGATOR TO PILOT

DO IT NOW

If any of your thoughts creates any tension, say YES, NO, MAYBE, NEVER, ALWAYS, SOMETIMES.

ALLOW YOUR MIND
TO
BECOME
YOUR PLAYGROUND

Begin to LET go INTO YOURSELF. Greet SHAME, as you meet HER, embrace HER with a HUG.

Begin to LET GO OUTSIDE YOURSELF. Greet SHAME, and allow the feeling to DISSOLVE through you.

MAYBE NEVER
SOMETIMES ALWAYS

As you have noticed, this book is designed to break TRANCE through TRANCE.

Learning to Live Your Trances — — — — —

CALL IN YOUR LOANS!

YOUR TRANCES TAKE CONTROL

SAVING FACE BEARS NO INTEREST

STOP
LETTING
OTHER
PEOPLE
PUT
YOU
UNDER

GO ON STRIKE
BECOME SUCCESSFUL

TAKE A CHANCE AND BREAK YOUR TRANCE

WHEN YOU REMEMBER THAT YOU HAVE FORGOTTEN WHO YOU PICKED TO DEFINE YOU, THE FEELING OF FULL OF AWE BEGINS TO DIMINISH. ANGER AND RESENTMENT LEAVE, AND YOU BEGIN TO REMEMBER
WHAT IT IS TO LIKE SOMEONE/YOURSELF FOR WHO/YOU ARE.

IT IS AWEFULL TO FEEL AWEFULL

FULL OF AWE IS PLEASANT

When we are full of awe, we can begin to feel aweful of what we are in awe of, when we forget that WE are DOING the DEFINING.

"Being Made To Feel Aweful" -- IS another Form of Controlling People Non-Violently. We are first taught the feeling of AWE as infants when the CONTEXT of Inherent A-SYM-A-Tree is auto-matic ALLY thrust on us. As this was NON-VERBAL we believe that to continue to feel FULL OF AWE is NECESSARY.

◆◆◆◆◆◆◆◆◆◆◆◆◆◆◆◆◆◆◆◆◆◆◆◆◆◆◆◆◆◆◆◆

Begin TO Create AWE THROUGH Your own CHOICE

◆◆◆◆◆◆◆◆◆◆◆◆◆◆◆◆◆◆◆◆◆◆◆◆◆◆◆◆◆◆◆◆

As you go DEEPER into YOUR trance, remember YOU are in control. LET go Deeper NOW -- INTO YOUR controlled trance of AWE.

NOT READY TO LET GO — — NOW

When you decide that it is time -- SHAME yourself into AWE.

 BUT NOT UNTIL THEN 

SOMETIMES NEVER
MAYBE ALWAYS

Many of us feel aweful. The feeling of AWE-FULL is frequently a result of asymmetry.

Awe—FULL, FULL of AWE is not the same thing as feeling aweful, although the mechanism of ONE-UP and ONE-DOWN is similar.

When we feel aweful in relation to others, we have in TRANCE--DEFINED the other as having A POWER over us. What this means is that we have chosen another person to define us as:

GOOD —————————— BAD
WORTHWHILE —————————— WORTHLESS

If it is time, quit your job, leave your husband, move. Your choices are your preferences. In the end you will turn out WELL DONE!

YOU MAY NOTICE A BLINK — — A TWITCH
YOUR HAND MAY MOVE UP OR DOWN OR
GET RELAXED

TENSION IN THE BACK?
MOVING IN YOUR SEAT
FLOATING IN BED

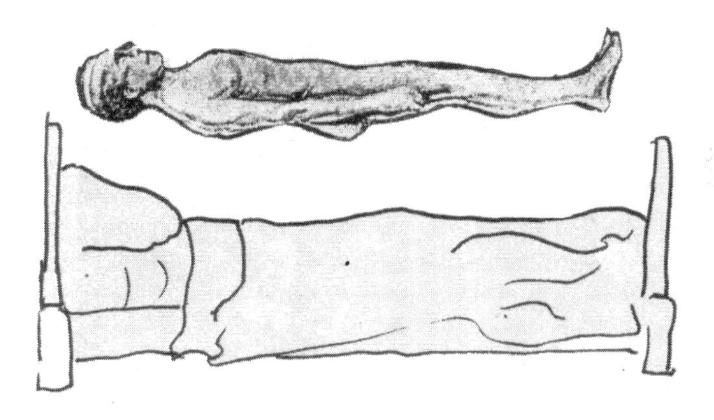

Find your leg with either hand. Notice the space between the contact?

YES ☐ NO ☐ MAYBE ☐

Charles Osgood was a genius in 1957. Do you remember SEMANTIC SPACE?

REMEMBER — — — SERFS UP

GO ON STRIKE AGAINST SLAVERY
BECOME SUCCESSFUL
WORK FOR YOURSELF

TAKE A CHANCE AND BREAK YOUR TRANCE

STOP LETTING OTHER PEOPLE
PUT YOU
UNDER

BECOME YOUR OWN HYPNOTIST

Now Dr. Hyatt, This is no way to write a book, or right a wrong. Come On, show them your real stuff. UP UP and AWAY!

The World of BEING is the Philosopher's Heaven

and Man's Hell

Final causes have been the curse of mankind. An invention of the mind to survive the phenomenal world? The mind has a tendency to think in opposites, thus creating the world of BEING. As our world consists of frustration, pain, struggles and death, the world of BEING therefore must consist of its opposite: immortality, pleasure and bliss. Would we require the world of BEING if we felt more powerful and were immortal?

APPLY HERE FOR EN - - - - - TRANCE

The way to success in any system is to know what fictions it chooses as its final cause(s).

Thus to answer "For The Good Of Mankind" is the correct answer, as you are lining your pockets with other people's gold.

If you answer, "For The Good Of Myself" while you are helping other people to find their gold, you have answered incorrectly.

If you can prove that your means leads to the proper ends, then you have won the case. Thus the purpose of lawyers.

As the mind prefers opposites to degrees on scales, it appears self-evident to the mind that the world of BEING exists. As far as we know, all that exists behind the apparent world is the world of raw sensation.

Why Do People Prefer To Seek Truth Rather Than Error? Could This Be A Function Of Ideology?

Within each ideal lurks the seed of its own destruction.

If we seek the ideal of Truth, we find the Error of the Ideal, says Freddie.

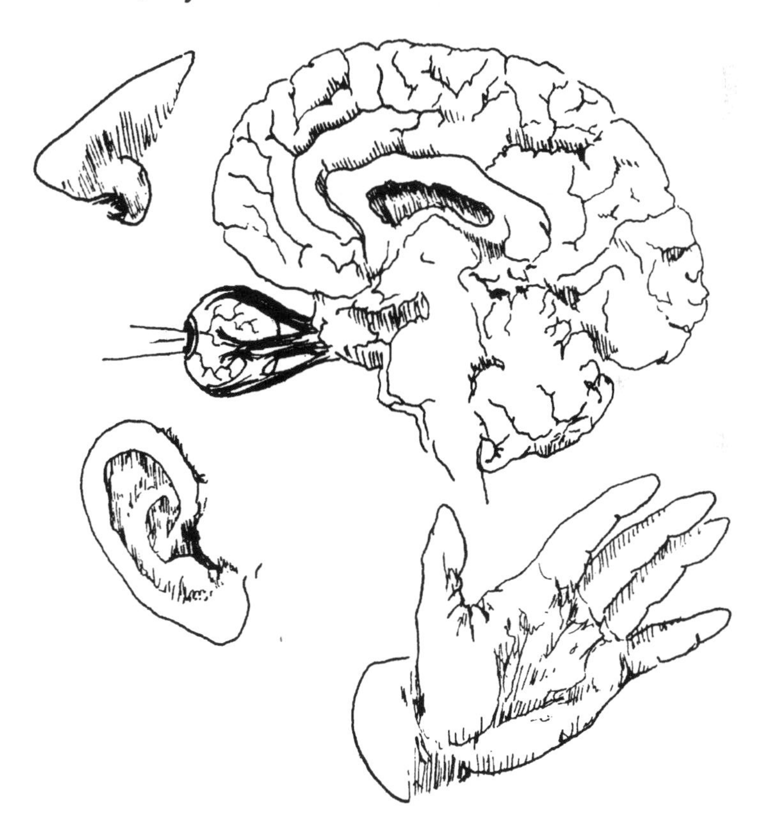

New tech: hedonic, represents an instrumental philosophy; the philosophy of altruism holds that the end can never justify the means. These seemingly contradictory and opposing forces, when received over and over again by YOUNG Farber-Silicone-Mush, insinuate a destructive
split creating
a house
divided
AGAINST
ITSELF.

Dis-obedience
is
the
only
CRIME!

The HISTORY of MANKIND is The HISTORY of

DUELING DOGMAS

DUALS are the result of ARM–CHAIR philosophers CORRALLING Living begins through language.

Language is the Primal MONOTHEISTIC GOD, who is worshipped by EVERYONE. Instead of Language serving us, WE serve and worship Language.

YOU ARE
HOW YOU USE LANGUAGE

We are tortured by the words we speak.
We are tortured by the words spoken to us.
Almost all of our experiences, most emotions and thoughts are the result of LANGUAGE worship. "Them are fighting WORDS, Boy."

MULTIPLE CHOICE TEST
Which One Are You?

Slow on the draw, but quick on the trigger.
Quick on the draw, but slow on the trigger.
Slow on the draw, but slow on the trigger.
Quick on the draw, but quick on the trigger.

OR

Are you unarmed?

Do you see yourself as unarmed, but do others see you as armed?

Do you dislike the metaphor of ARMS?

BLANK--Fill in your own questions and answers.

The above questionnaire provides you with a unique opportunity to study yourself in a way which few people do.

Most humans are either unable or refuse to see how they affect other people. Our own sense of power over ourselves and the world is a TABOO TOPIC.

DUELISM IS THE RESULT OF LANGUAGE AND NOT A RESULT OF "FACT."

Are you a body or a mind?
Are you a result of nature or nurture?
Christian or Jew or?

THE LANGUAGE CONVEYOR BELT

The stages of life, from CRADLE TO GRAVE. Did you make all these choices?

BLANK

CONCEPTION

GESTATION

BLANK

BIRTH

TOILET TRAINING

BLANK

MOM & POP

Religion

Country

Blank

School

Blank

University

Insurance

Jobs

Mates

Families

Blank

Burial

Death

Grave

BLANKS

After all of the above, do you expect me to take you seriously? Must I respect YOUR RIGHTS to YOUR DOGMA? YOUR CHOICES AND BELIEFS?

— — SOLUTION — — JUMP — — TO ANOTHER CONVEYOR BELT? NO

WORDS KILL AMMUNITION FOR THE FOOL

Buy a dictionary, study law, Bibble slavery, Babble, correct the Language hair professor.

DO YOU SHOOT FROM THE HIP?
DRAW AND SHOOT YOURSELF IN THE LEG?
DRAW AND AIM?

DOES LANGUAGE CREATE PROBLEMS WHICH DO NOT EXIST?

NO EXPERTS PLEASE
NO COMMITTEE
MEETINGS

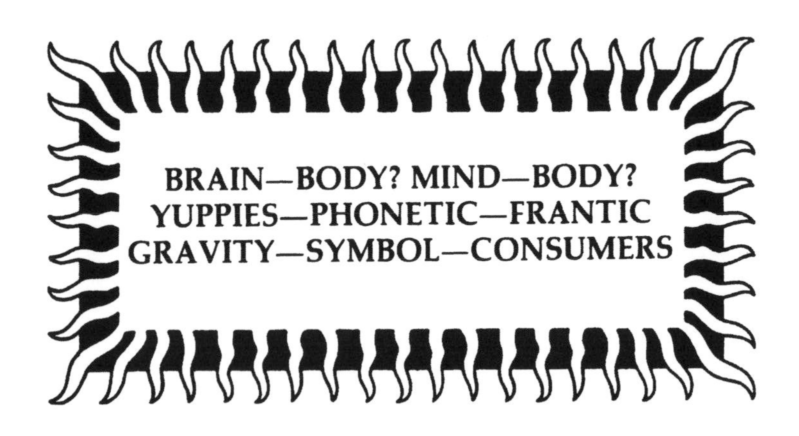

BRAIN—BODY? MIND—BODY?
YUPPIES—PHONETIC—FRANTIC
GRAVITY—SYMBOL—CONSUMERS

We use words to convey how things operate. As such, words dissect atoms in motion/process. As such they are, at best, an approximate description of how things really work.

Words are also used to express hopes, needs, wants, emotions, motions. When we use words this way, they reflect ideology.

Ideologies are the goals and objectives that influence individuals and whole cultures.

An ideologist is a person or group who is an expert in formulating visions, often forced on you to live as your nightmare...zzzzzz.

An Ideologist is skilled in using language to please and persuade.

This includes the art of affected speech and exaggeration in selling a particular illusion.

The ideologist uses language to affect groups and individuals to support Hir hallucination.

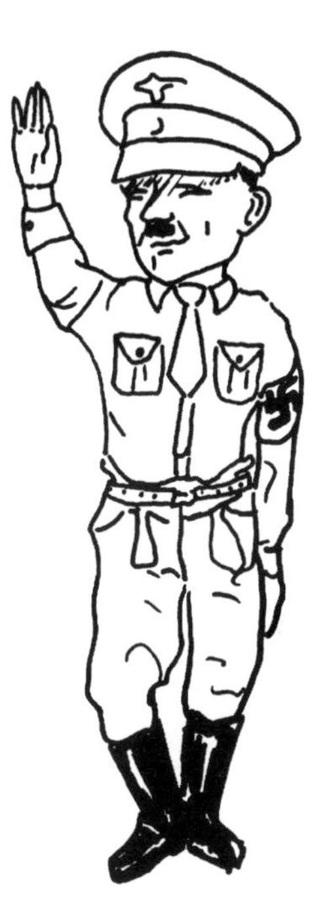

The method is quite simple. All humans are dissatisfied with something. Tell them that they are more dissatisfied than they are, provide them with any solution which fits your needs, and then tacitly or directly tell them to do certain things to accomplish the goal. Create mystery, enemies, identifiable slogans, stage a few events, etc. The important point to remember: what the group does in NO WAY has to relate to the original dissatisfaction or the proposed solution.

$$HCl + HNO_3$$

◆◆◆◆◆◆◆◆◆◆◆◆◆◆◆◆◆◆◆◆◆◆◆◆◆◆◆◆◆◆◆◆◆◆◆◆◆◆

THE FRAUD FOR THE YOUNG LION IS TEACHING IT TO BELIEVE THAT IT NO LONGER NEEDS ITS CLAWS AND TEETH— THAT THE JACKAL AND HIDE WILL PREPARE ITS MEAL.

(Hyatt reflecting on the need of the State)

◆◆◆◆◆◆◆◆◆◆◆◆◆◆◆◆◆◆◆◆◆◆◆◆◆◆◆◆◆◆◆◆◆◆◆◆◆◆

Hyatt's Method

is *purely* **practical**

Find Your True

Temper-

ments

& learn

to be lived by them

While Hyatt

under **[stands]**

the mind's

Need

for metaphysics

his technique is to

Always

lie down

under **[neath]** *it*

In this way

He is able to

Sniff Out

the Joy or Pain

which supports it.

INTENTION and/or DEFINITION

CAN TRANSFORM

ACCIDENT

into a

HEROIC ACT or a CRIME

WILL and DESIRE

It seems that again we are faced with a struggle, a necessary one, albeit. Will is intention, or as some authors believe, will is a form of Fate-ESSENCE, DNA wired in destiny if you WILL. There is a quality to Will which brings forth colors as BLUE, GREY, OR MayBe WHITE.

Desire is hotter than Will, with colours like Red and Orange. Sometimes there is an organic tone to desire, as in the case of reproduction and then a GREEN might be mixed in for good measure.

The classical conflict between Will and Desire goes something like this:

ROUND ONE

"I'd like that piece of pie."

"No, you're too fat and diabetic."

ROUND TWO

"The hell with it, I'll give in. It's good to give in once in a while."

"That sounds like a rationalization. And although what you say is true, this is not one of those times."

There are many possible scenarios for this daily drama. The attentive reader will note that the so-called WILL was really an internalized authority figure, and in fact had nothing to do with Will at all. If this person would say that they had no real Will-Power, we would disagree. They seem to defeat the authority figure at one level, and always lose at another. This is one reason why habits are so hard to break. The "desire" to break them is imposed on the subject by an internalized object-figure.

This type of struggle is hopeless lest the person separate herself from the conflict and recognize that it is a struggle between WILLS. (The child's will IS desire, and the adult Will is NO.) This is the struggle of a victim, until the introjected parent or authority is replaced by the person's own WILLS.

My desire is to Will, and I am willing my desire. Once this Sin-Tax is broken apart and seen clearly, YOU can eat your pie or not. Until that time "you" doesn't exist in any real sense.

"I desire to Will not to eat Pie now."

"I will my desire to eat Pie now."

ROUND THREE

"That's right, I'll wait til later."

"Look, the answer is NO."

ROUND FOUR

"Whose life is it anyway? This is what I want to do. It is my Will to eat it. If I get sick, so I'll have to pay for it. Besides, I don't like being told what to do."

ROUND FIVE

"I feel awful. I shouldn't have eaten the pie. I'll do better tomorrow. I won't eat it again."

YOUR WILL TRUE DESIRED

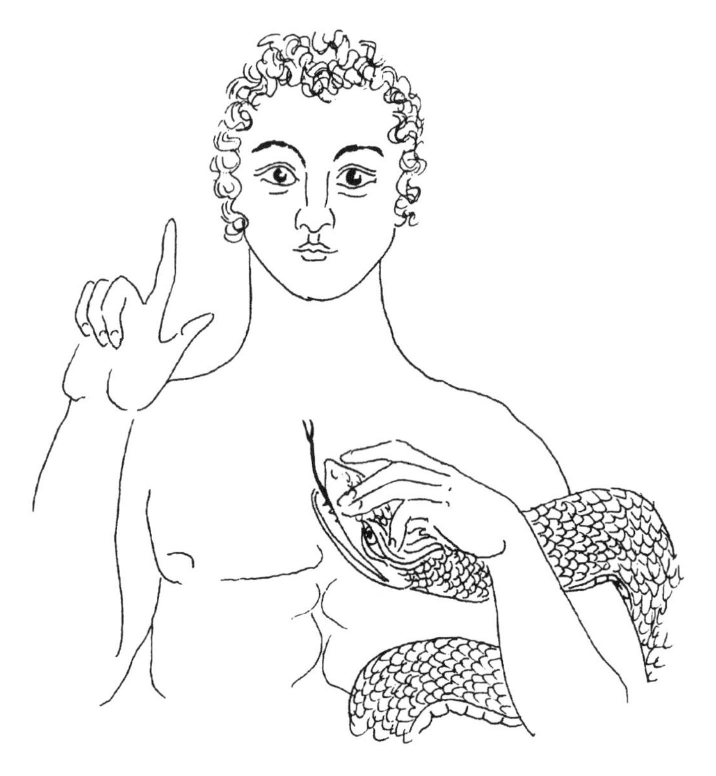

If you say this with complete concentration—follow-through is simultaneous. There is no false split, nor a false struggle, as YOU are DOING your Desire/WILL/DESIRE/Will.

If you desire you can be in charge, if you will you can have your desire. These are not just words, but a technique which creates:

YOUR TRUE WILL DESIRED RESULTS

STOP SHOOTING BLANKS

STARS SHINE
even when it's
CLOUDY

The New Being is no longer waiting in the wings...
...SHe's now in your head.

"Then Dear Dr. Hyatt, what is the problem?"

"The problem, dear sir, is letting yourself know that no matter what you do, you are the producer, director, leading WoMan, supporting caste, audience, ticket taker, etc. YOU ARE THE SHOW.

"The next problem, dear sir, is accepting that no matter who a person is and no matter how much they might deny it, they are also the producer, director, leading WoMan, supporting caste, audience, ticket taker, etc. THEY ARE THE SHOW.

"The final problem, sir, after learning all of the above, is knowing how to be a bit player in other people's shows while still remembering that you are the Star.

"When everyone knows that they can't be anything but the Star, then Intelligence will increase geometrically on the Planet earth. People will no longer need to fight for the starring role."

YOUR CONTROL MAKES TRANCES
ONLY LET GO WHEN YOU CHOOSE!

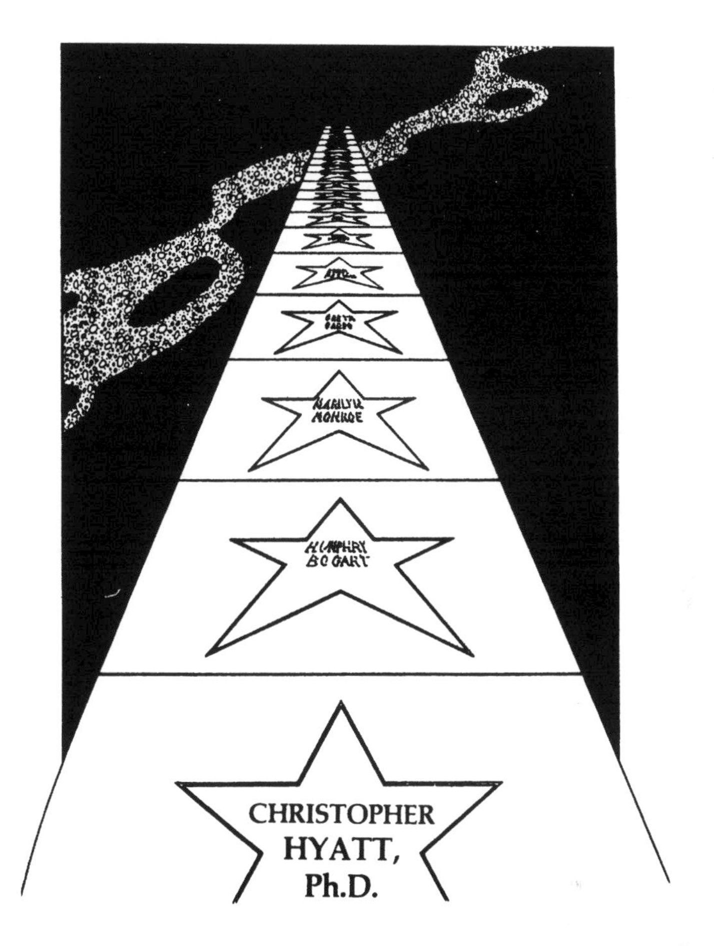

When someone doesn't understand that you are a Star, do not forget to remember to SMI^{2}LE.

Many people need to be told by others that they are a very important Star. Tell them in a way that they can understand, using their own trance techniques.

One reason why some people need to be told so frequently that they are a Star is that they refuse to accept that they are a Star. You can not convey the right message to them unless you enter their trance – re – liberately them.

As we learned early in the game, MONOTHEISM is the refusal to accept the principle that:

Every Man And Every Woman Is A Star

No matter what role you play in the Game of Life you are a Star. Even followers are in the Lead.

IT IS IMPOSSIBLE NOT TO BE YOUR OWN CENTER

There is no-Self to find, nothing was ever lost, you can't give yourself away no matter what you do.

As you begin to re-read the preceding few paragraphs, become aware of your body twitching. Somewhere deep inside someone is Shaking Yes. As you begin to realize this idea and free yourself from anything which forces you into an unpleasant place, you may begin to find a greater number of choices available to you.

When you begin to facilitate your own options, you will also become acutely aware how your own freedom allows you to become more expressive and creative in playing different parts.

YOU ARE THE CASTING DIRECTOR

AND NOW STARRING

The Final Words of A WESTERN MASTER

Interviewed by Christopher S. Hyatt, Ph.D.

HYATT: This interview is going to be tough.

REGARDIE: Yes—I find myself resisting it. Every time I open my mouth I appear to get into some sort of trouble.

HYATT: Yes. You're an iconoclast. Let's start with something easy.

REGARDIE: All right; I'm game.

HYATT: When did you start writing The Complete Golden Dawn System of Magic?

REGARDIE: Somewhere around 1979 or so. My memory is not quite clear as to the exact date. But it was about then that I wrote my first synopsis of what should be included.

HYATT: What made you take on such a monumental project?

REGARDIE: (Laughing) It's rather difficult to say. (I've had a couple of Bloody Marys!) Well—my reasons for writing it were manifold. I will describe a couple of the more simple motives that I don't mind making public. Others are more personal, so I'll keep them private for the time being.

The first exposition, written over forty years ago, was hastily thrown together. It was incomplete in all sorts of ways. In those days I was more impulsive or more impatient than I am now. There were whole areas which should have been elaborated, but which were not clarified at all. Some very important Golden Dawn documents were also omitted—even though my original intention was to make the book as complete as I could.

A very dear friend of mine, Carr P. Collins, Jr. of Dallas [Texas], was good enough to obtain, in 1979, a complete set of Golden Dawn documents from the late Gerald Yorke in England. He gave me enormous encouragement and moral support. This then provided the opportunity of realizing how much had been omitted and how much could be reedited. On studying this new set of documents I decided to ensure that *The Complete Golden Dawn System of Magic* would be a much more complete version of the Order's teaching than the original hastily-put-together version was.

One of the things that has always rankled me is human secrecy. So long as this body of knowledge remains locked up in one or more human being's brains, it runs the risk of being lost to mankind forever. It needs to be put in book form to be distributed all over the world, so that if some type of cataclysm occurred someone, somewhere, would be able to rediscover this material and once more make it available. So long as a few books can be found tucked away somewhere, this knowledge cannot be lost. So, therefore, in writing *The Complete Golden Dawn System of Magic* my intention was to make it as complete as possible, hoping that Falcon Press would make certain that this had the widest possible distribution. Thus, in the event that there was a major calamity, and Western civilization as we know it was destroyed in the Northern hemisphere, there would be dozens or hundreds of sets of this teaching distributed in the Southern hemisphere. Then this form of occult knowledge, this particular rendition of being "brought to the Light," would endure for another thousand years or so.

HYATT: Do you then see a disaster of these proportions occurring in the next few decades?

REGARDIE: Yes, I suspect something of that type occurring. But for the moment, let's go to something else.

HYATT: How did you meet Carr?

REGARDIE: It went something like this. He was involved with a small study group in Dallas, studying *The Tree of Life* and *The Golden Dawn.* The first seemed pretty obscure. The group was mostly concerned with the problem of pronouncing the Hebrew words. So out of the blue, he wrote me a letter care of my then publishers. "We want to learn how to pronounce these words. Can you help us?" At that time it hadn't occurred to me to dictate a tape. Anyway, I didn't have a tape recorder then; this was in the early 60s, some twenty years ago, though I did have a wire recorder. In answering him, I suggested that all he had to do was to enquire at the nearest Hebrew synagogue or temple for this information. "They won't burn you, they won't cook you, they won't do anything awful to you. Just say that you have your group interested in the Qabalah (they won't understand in the least; perhaps they'll think you're crazy), and you want to learn the pronunciation of certain Hebrew words and names. They will either say "Get the hell out of here" or else "Look, we've got a young man here who will be glad to help." So that's the letter I wrote to Carr. I never heard another word. About a year later I was fiddling around with my files and came across this letter of his with the notes that I had made. So I wrote him another letter. I asked, "What happened? Did you take my counsel and go to a local temple and find out how these words are pronounced?" His reply was, "No. We did nothing of the kind. Why don't you come down here and give us a course?" At first this sounded preposterous to me. But he again wrote me a letter and asked would I come? Not really wanting to do this, I thought I would be a real smart ass and said, Yes, I'll come, naming what I then thought a preposterous fee for one day; my fee will be $500.00 plus all expenses. And damn it, he went for that! So I couldn't back out. I never thought anybody would be extravagant enough to offer me $500.00 for that. So anyway, that's how I met Carr and the relationship has been good since. There were a couple of amusing differences in the meantime about that. He said, "Fine, come down to Dallas and in the evening after the lecture, we'll pick your brains." I was a might hackled at that. I said, "Now look, if I come down to lecture, or whatever it is, for two days, I'll give you everything I can during the daytime, but after dinner, or when my hours are up, I don't want anybody around me. Leave me alone!" So that put an end to his notion that they were just going to sit around and have a nice long conversation all evening. In other words I would not be obliged to talk for 48 hours continuously.

HYATT: I guess they still gained a lot.

REGARDIE: I hope so. They were very, very nice people. A good group whom I came to love and respect. That's why I appreciate his latest letter, that if I ever move to Dallas there would be a nice nucleus of friends. Anyway that's the way it happened. So from that day he's been very sympathetic, very generous and understanding and a good sounding board. He could occasionally provoke a series of questions that I hadn't let's say, spontaneously considered, which was most evocative or stimulating.

HYATT: Did you feel his was a rather prosaic point of view?

REGARDIE: Not really. He was a very warm, practical person, very pragmatic. I like him enormously. You've got a totally different kind of mind altogether, more analytical.

HYATT: Well—I do know that I prefer experience to long drawn out theories or explanations. I'm the kind of person that prefers the experience rather than the explanation of the experience. Of course, I have been trained to think in a scientific and analytic fashion. Sometimes perhaps it gets in the way.

REGARDIE: I doubt it. Your analytic mind is OK.

HYATT: Thanks. But I prefer religious and therapeutic orientations which are more experiential than theoretical. Too much theory always disturbs me. I know we've talked about this before. The lack of life in many of the people who have gotten into the occult. Many of them have become sort of dead. They lose their sex life, they lose their party life, and a lot of them lose all spontaneity. In fact, I doubt if many of them have much life at all.

REGARDIE: You're right. They probably never had much real life to them. This picture however extends more or less over this whole occult field, a sort of moral miasma.

HYATT: What makes me feel good is when I see some of the Bhagwan Rajneesh's followers. They are out there dancing and yelling and...

REGARDIE: Yes, that's great. Darned good idea.

HYATT: They are doing something. Even those with an intellectual background—they are active and alive. My nature demands the catharsis—the doing. The image of the librarian sitting in a vast room with millions of books turns me off. To me this is not the study of the occult! I like the Golden Dawn System because it demands something more experiential than the intellect.

REGARDIE: Yes, this is why I like it, too. Anyway, I am not that intellectual. I *can* be, but I have more of a sense of the whole structure rather than a deep intellectual understanding.

HYATT: That's right. You have a good grasp of the whole field and of the people in it. Are we getting into trouble yet?

REGARDIE: Yes we are. (Laughter) If we've got to use another word, which still requires a lot of explanation, I have an intuitive perception of some of the essence of this material.

HYATT: Yes. And I think that has more to offer than someone who can delve into every vowel and consonant.

REGARDIE: That's why we still need librarians to balance people like you and me.

HYATT: However, you have people like Waite (who are librarians of the most dogmatic kind) who have had or attract the kind of audience that we're talking about, a very moralistic, staid, old-fashioned, non-expressive, non-orgasmic...

REGARDIE: Yes, non-orgasmic in nature. It's the old Christian morality again. He was steeped in that. And he attracted those few people who were already steeped in it like him. Anybody else would have loathed him.

HYATT: Yes! If they had a sense of their own being they probably would. Remember that time we were in a Boulder bookstore and this girl started to talk about how stiff Regardie's writings were compared to Waite! She didn't recognize you, of course, and you in jest agreed with her.

REGARDIE: Yes, that was very funny. If I thought that my work was as stiff and straight-laced as his I would soon shoot myself. (Laughter)

HYATT: Waite sure wouldn't fit in well with a guy like you, or Crowley or Rajneesh or anyone who was pro-life. I imagine that some people who have read your works can't imagine you having a lot of fun and driving around in a sports car at the age of 77.

REGARDIE: We are getting in trouble again, but what you said is sad but true. This is one reason why I generally avoid people in this field. They can't integrate the fact that someone like me can have a lot of fun—and be simply ordinary in so many ways. They expect of me a certain role and become disappointed when they find me so different from their expectations.

HYATT: Isn't that always a problem in the occult...that a weird separation is made between the spiritual and the material. I find that very annoying.

REGARDIE: You're lucky. You haven't had that early orientation which separates them.

HYATT: No, I never had.

REGARDIE: You're so lucky in that sense. I grew up, as it were, in a theosophical milieu. I discovered it (theosophy) too early which was a great mistake. As a result of that, Blavatsky imprinted her moral dichotomy on me. Or let's say I was ready for the imprinting (I can't blame it on the old girl). Obviously I did reject a great deal of that by moving towards Crowley. Yet in many ways I'm still prosaic.

HYATT: Then you rejected it again by moving towards Reich.

REGARDIE: Yes, but that was much later, about 1950. But there was the earlier revolt against her rigid morality by gravitating towards Crowley which none of the rest of my theosophical family would have done. Or could have done. Poor Crowley had to live with my adolescent stiffness. He prodded me, but he was really very gentle and understanding to this 20 year old kid. I owe so much to him. Crowley never saw the material as contrary to the spiritual. This may be one reason he is not liked.

HYATT: Didn't Eddy say poverty was a disease?

REGARDIE: Eddy?

HYATT: Mary Baker.

REGARDIE: She's right! It took me a long time to appreciate that old girl. I never really appreciated her until I wrote *The Romance of Metaphysics* in 1939–40 [since republished as the *Teachers of Fulfillment*]. Even then, I didn't really appreciate what she said until probably 12 years ago.

HYATT: What about her thing about not giving drugs to children when they were ill?

REGARDIE: Oh that's overdoing it. Fanaticism of the worst kind. When kids had polio she kept saying that everything would be fine. Because in her mind the physical body didn't really exist, it was only an illusion.

She was crazy as all hell. But once you get her basic ideas in your bonnet of what she stood for however, it follows in a kind of logical sequence. A kind of illogical-logic.

HYATT: If the physical body doesn't exist, why bother giving anything to it?

REGARDIE: But the funny thing is, she knew that was a farce...because she loved money. And if the things of this world were unreal, why crave them?

The problem with people who read Eddy, and the people who read Crowley, or Jesus or Rajneesh or you or anyone else, is that they don't see the various sides of the author's personalities. They sort of choose one facet that they want to see. It is a sad thing.

HYATT: Yes, they have to see only one facet. Just one facet. I guess they try to make whole pictures out of things which are not wholes in the real world sense. One body—therefore one personality, etc. This is why so many people have problems with themselves. This attitude doesn't lead one to have much hope for the human race in its present form.

REGARDIE: That we know. It doesn't say much for the human race; they can't handle this sort of thing. Now we are really getting into trouble. (Laughter) Look at what they did to Reich!

Let's get back to Eddy. Apart from anything else, the old girl really was an amazing woman. The thing that I marvel at, since we know how difficult it is to change behavior patterns; here's a woman who was a failure, sick, rejected, a total failure up to the age of 60, and to make a turn-about at 60, I think is a real bloody miracle. So that's where she fits in as far as I'm concerned, with the whole notion of the magical and mystical experience which somehow changes a non-entity into an entity. Something must have happened to her—what? But whatever it was, it transformed her and made her into a dynamo. There are a lot of silly explanations floating about, but I don't believe most of them.

HYATT: Did her transformation stop her from being frightened?

REGARDIE: No, she was always frightened actually. She would go through these periods of let's say hysterical seizures, in which she'd have real paranoid notions that she was being attacked by malicious animal magnetism, which is a pure paranoid delusion. Her only safeguard against that, was to surround herself with all the faithful disciples she could muster. They would pray, and deny that there was any such thing as malicious animal magnetism. And this went on all her life. If you take the position that there is only goodness and light in the world then by her logic all else is an illusion, body included.

HYATT: But she couldn't really believe that?

REGARDIE: Well she did, theoretically. Only in theory, and then only to a limited extent. She transformed her life by this theory. But she was still subject to the same set of delusions.

HYATT: Freudian repressions, would you say?

REGARDIE: Yes. Which every now and then would bubble up. Something would happen as a prompt or stimulus and up they would come. And she was helpless. But it was labeled Animal Magnetism. God help any person in her environment on whom she put that label. They would really be persecuted, driven out from the flock.

HYATT: Exiled, I bet, to California. (Laughter) What's Animal Magnetism—by her definition?

REGARDIE: Somebody who directs a stream of evil thoughts which were probably all about sex (laughter) ...Most of her disciples were pure virginal maidens all afraid of their tails; this was malicious animal magnetism. A guy like you or me (ha!) would come along and make them aware of their sexual streamings and that's malicious animal magnetism. (Laughter) They would have to get rid of you immediately.

HYATT: So she wouldn't have gotten along with Crowley very well?

REGARDIE: (Laughter) You are really funny. Oh, no. He wouldn't have gotten along very well with her either! He wouldn't have gotten near her.

HYATT: How do you explain the split that some people in the occult have about sex and spirituality?

REGARDIE: Rather as Freud would explain it.

HYATT: You don't see such a split between the spirit and sex.

REGARDIE: No. None at all.

HYATT: I don't think most people in the occult or the metaphysical field would share that with you.

REGARDIE: No. But that's because they're not aware of the basic Freudian mechanisms or theories. Nor can they observe the operation of these mechanisms in themselves.

HYATT: Or the demonstrations of Reich, either.

REGARDIE: Oh, it's the same thing. One has to identify Reich with Freud. One is an evolution from the other. They're both rooted in the same ground, but neither of them would admit it. That's the abysmal stupidity of this whole field, too.

HYATT: Does this explain why you don't want to bother with most people in the occult and psychology fields?

REGARDIE: In a very large measure. As soon as they begin to talk it's offensive to me.

HYATT: In which way?

REGARDIE: Cosmic Foo-Foo. Flying saucers, star seeds, or whatever kind of crazy nonsense. All the stuff that's pure projection of their own need structures. Occasionally I will go to an occult bookstore here or there and browse around. I just listen to people talk. I don't say anything. Sometimes I may strike up a conversation to get them going. They don't recognize me—that is until now, with all these photos you've published. I'll prod them, and just listen to the crap that follows. You see you have gotten me in trouble again.

HYATT: Are these type of people what you refer to as sweet and light?

REGARDIE: Yes, that and more. I would also call them lazy and infantile. They give the field a bad reputation. For them there is no evil, no lust, there is no nothing. They have the planes all mixed up. Everything changes by just wishing. Everything is nice, pure and holy, which is *au fond* but not in their sense of the words.

HYATT: Really they don't want to deal with anything.

REGARDIE: No. Nothing! They're happy all the time...

HYATT: Do you really think that?

REGARDIE: No! Of course not. They're an abysmal mess. An abysmal mess.

HYATT: That's probably one reason they don't like Crowley much.

REGARDIE: He would chew up this Cosmic Foo-Foo and spit it out. Crowley made so many enemies simply by talking about sex, violence, etc., the way he did. And let me add this, you're creating a whole lot of enemies for us now in the opening of *The Complete Golden Dawn System of Magic,* where you talk about sex. You will create a whole lot of enemies right away.

HYATT: Do you think we should take that section out?

REGARDIE: No. Those kinds of people don't belong to the true tradition of the Golden Dawn anyway.

HYATT: In what sense am I creating enemies?

REGARDIE: Because this strikes a mortal blow to the very core of their existence.

HYATT: How do you deal with that? You are a person who is, for lack of a better phrase, pro-sex, pro-life, etc.

REGARDIE: Yes, I like it.

HYATT: So here you are writing this material to a large group of people who, in essence, don't have the foggiest idea what you are talking about.

REGARDIE: There is always a forlorn hope that a seed will drop somewhere. After all, it dropped on me! God, when I was 16 I was an inhibited mess. And then I saw the name Blavatsky in a book and that did the trick. That moved me on to other things. I say, you know I've had a charmed life in one sense. I've never really had to make any great effort to be progressive. I know you don't agree with me on this point, but I still have to stick to my guns here and I must say this comes from a very deep conviction that I'm really a very ordinary kind of character who had the good fortune, the luck, the insanity, whatever, to hook his wagon to two stars, almost by accident and got whirled away with it and from there all these other things occurred without really any effort on my part.

HYATT: You might be ordinary in that sense, but a lot of people are ordinary and they never got whirled away nor do they do anything but live an ordinary life.

REGARDIE: (Laughter) I'm lucky. This is what I say, the Gods have been very kind to me, very kind.

I was lucky, that's all. It's like that lovely story about the guy who picks up a girl and takes her to his room. They begin to talk the next morning. "How come a nice girl like you is in this room with me? You are a graduate of Vassar, a Ph.D., wealthy, etc., how come?" She says, "Well, I'm just lucky." So I'm in the same boat. I have been pursued by good luck. Not because of anything I've done. Almost in spite of what I've done.

HYATT: Well, that's very rare.

REGARDIE: Yes, it is. I've been so lucky, or had good Karma. Occasionally things just drop into my lap. Look, let's be very personal. What could be more lucky than having you come along, 20 years ago to learn Reichian therapy from me? And now just look at us today. We are involved in so many things together.

HYATT: Can you talk further on your feeling of luck?

REGARDIE: Yes. From the point of view of just plain bloody good accidental luck, I'm one of the luckiest bastards in the world really. Here I am, originally a little Jewish non-entity who somehow, with a stroke of good luck, got into things he could never have dreamed of—never. And without any education. I had one semester of high school, and then went to school at night admittedly.

HYATT: Many occultists I've met have said, there's no such thing as luck! They believe that the person makes it all happen.

REGARDIE: All right. Let's say someone is a Buddhist, we can speak in terms of good Karma or merit. I must have accumulated good merit in the past that has finally paid off in the form of what we call good luck now.

HYATT: Do you buy that?

REGARDIE: Yes. Oh sure. Intrinsically. So even though I explain it in my English way, I'm a perfectly ordinary guy, who then got so whirled up, so accidentally, into another kind of spiritual activity.

HYATT: That will teach you to write letters to people like Crowley. (Laughter)

REGARDIE: Yes (still laughing), it took 18 months for my letter to get there. But it got there. Now that really is pure accident. I wrote him in 1927 at his publishers 13 years after they went out of business.

In the meantime World War I had occurred. He had wandered around all over the damn place. He had no permanent address. He was a wanderer.

HYATT: Like me?

REGARDIE: No, he was worse than you'll ever be. He coined the right phrase himself, he was "a wanderer of the wastes." He couldn't settle down. He always had to be moving. He was a bit like Carr is now. Nothing could make Carr settle down, nothing, but that's another story—it's his true will which is great. But Crowley was worse. You know accident and destiny are the same thing. I equate them. Karma, destiny, accident, it's unmistakable.

HYATT: I'd like to hear more about how you got started in all of this.

REGARDIE: My sister brought home some of her cultish books on diet and health. I saw the name Blavatsky in one of these books. She was unfortunately ridiculed by the whole family, but she really brought culture to the home. She brought music, books, etc. Actually I am deeply indebted to her. So what could be more accidental than opening up one of her cultish books and seeing "Blavatsky"? There were of course other names mentioned there—why that particular one? I think it was just an awakening of an old Karmic tie. And why Crowley? I was at a meeting one night with a lawyer who had a copy of Crowley's book on Yoga. He had a half a dozen adoring neophytes, you know, he was parading as the great, wise man. So we sat around listening to him read in his pretentious legal voice, from Crowley's book. Boy, it got me! It awakened a high enthusiasm in me. So I had to get the name of the book, the author, and the address. And the address was 13 to 14 years old! I wrote him a letter and went off to Philadelphia to study at the art school there. Eighteen months later a letter came from the old man in Paris, which said, "I have your letter, get in touch with my representative in New York." I did so immediately. All this is a fantastic story, really. Pure accident. Why I would have stumbled into this...bred as we all were, in this atmosphere of complete repression, inhibition, patriarchy, etc. How could I have come out of that into this weird bloody wonderful world...it's a miracle, that's all I can say. My life is a series of miracles that have occurred in the most haphazard "accidental" way.

HYATT: Let's switch topics for a moment.

REGARDIE: O.K. What would you like to talk about?

HYATT: Well...the "new" Christian movement.

REGARDIE: Oh that! More enemies. O.K. I originally thought that the movement had some promise. Having steeped myself in Christian mysticism, my thought was when I first heard of the movement, that there was a revival taking place in Christian mysticism. And that's when I began to investigate. It took only a short while to realize it was completely hollow. It was a purely hysterical eruption.

HYATT: It also seems very patriarchal and authoritarian.

REGARDIE: Well, see it as the eruption of all their father images. Of course it's totally authoritarian. One of the weird things about it though, (and this is so funny), I never got one of them to explain this to me. The Pentecostals, the real originators of all this born-again stuff never celebrated Christmas. Apparently they believe that Christmas is a pagan holiday and not truly Christian.

HYATT: So you spent some time investigating that organization?

REGARDIE: Oh yes. About a year or so, hoping that there might be some real element of revival of the old ecstasies of St. John of the Cross, St. Theresa and other mystics.

HYATT: In the gnostic tradition?

REGARDIE: They'd die a million deaths rather than think of that.

HYATT: How long do you think this movement will last?

REGARDIE: So long as there are repressed and split people this movement will endure in one form or another; it always has. It's only in the last 100 years that it has been called Pentecostal. You know the lovely vision of St. Anthony, he was always tormented by visions of the devil and naked women, etc., so you know what was on his mind. They were basket cases, preoccupied with sin and the devil.

HYATT: Don't you see any redemption in trying to be master of the flesh?

REGARDIE: No. When confronted by temptation, yield. (Laughter)

HYATT: And that's the only way to redemption? (Laughter)

REGARDIE: Right. St. Paul said, "Shall we sin in order to be saved?" and he said no, but the answer is really yes! (Laughter) For how else can you be saved? Otherwise there is no point in salvation. But seriously for a moment, the flesh must be dealt with but not through any of the silly techniques provided by the current religions. And it must not be mastered on moral grounds, but simply on the functional grounds of wanting to be more than human. Lastly, for it to be mastered, it must first be fulfilled and respected; no repression, no denial, no punishment, no nonsense.

HYATT: I have a question. What is evil?

REGARDIE: From the Christian point of view, evil is your body, your sex drive. Sex is the beginning and the end of evil, as in the Adam and Eve story—original sin.

HYATT: But what is it from the more enlightened point of view? What is evil?

REGARDIE: Damned if I know. (Laughter) It gets into black and white magic... We were talking about that earlier over dinner. If you're doing something for yourself it's black magic. If you're doing something for someone else it's white magic. That to me sounds very silly. So if you're trying to improve yourself, then it's black magic, right? The whole idea of evil as it is commonly used is crazy. By the way, is there a grey magic?

HYATT: You recommended psycho-therapy for those people seeking to embark on the Great Work. It seems that most people don't pay any attention to your advice.

REGARDIE: Absolutely. But never mind whether they pay attention, I'll still insist on it. You see it is the only valid requirement for a sane occultism.

HYATT: What school of therapy?

REGARDIE: I don't care. Any school.

HYATT: Jungian?

REGARDIE: Even that. Once they've been exposed to even a little bit of it, it's like a virus, like herpes, it takes root.

HYATT: I feel that therapy doesn't get deep enough.

REGARDIE: I agree with you, but it makes a beginning, that's all I'm concerned with. As long as some entry can be made into their armor somewhere along the road, then it's all to the good. The rest will happen, by happenstance, Karma, accident, call it whatever you will.

HYATT: At least we can hope for that.

REGARDIE: I think we can count on it. I will. It may not show immediately, but after some years it will. Look what it's done for your friend. Your description of him was that he is almost human! Miracles do happen. Any kind of therapy I think is absolutely essential for someone in this field, because as a rule they have absolutely no insight whatsoever. Now if they've been slightly oriented to the Crowley point of view, they're a wee bit different. But they can still be completely balmy.

HYATT: What type of therapy is best from your point of view?

REGARDIE: Listen, I have my own experience of therapy. I had one year of Jungian, two years of Freudian, four years of Reichian. There is no comparison between them. The year of Jungian was a wasted year. The only thing it did for me, and this is the most important thing, it made me delve into Jungian literature. I became conversant with the lingo. It gave me a philosophy which still has its place in my life, but as therapy I think it's utterly useless. And all this business of active imagination and making an image of a figure in a dream and talking to it is plain mental masturbation.

HYATT: A lot of them say it's similar to skrying.

REGARDIE: There's a difference.

HYATT: How would you differentiate?

REGARDIE: Well, you've got a technique for dealing with the skrying to make sure it's not your imagination, to make sure that it's not delusion; you've got a technique for dealing with it.

HYATT: In The Complete Golden Dawn?

REGARDIE: Yes, sure. It's in the critique I wrote for the section on skrying. It didn't come over on the computer disk at first, but I think it's a pretty good critique.

HYATT: Yes, I got that in the mail and I will process that.

REGARDIE: Yes, that you've got to do. That's an important part of the whole business, I'd hate to have that omitted.

HYATT: Colin Wilson recently said that he regarded you as the last living representative of the great occult tradition of the late 19th century, whose names included Blavatsky, Yeats, Mathers, Waite, Crowley and Dion Fortune. Also Francis King gave you credit for the revival of the esoteric tradition in the 1960s. Before you start shaking your head, Alan Watts and people like Leary and Wilson credit your work as having made a great contribution to the higher consciousness revolution. What are your feelings about these statements?

REGARDIE: I'll accept the statement of King's and maybe that of Watts, Wilson and Leary. Yes, that I'll accept. I will say that's unequivocal. The other statement of placing me in the category of H.P.B. etc., this is a considerable exaggeration. I would like to believe that that's true, but in all common sense there isn't any justification. Blavatsky and Crowley are in a category all by themselves; leave out Yeats who I think is a lesser figure where this area is concerned. He may have been a considerable poet, but there is nothing in his history to indicate his great command of the magical tradition. Arthur Machen was another non-entity in this area too, though he was a very great novelist, and so forth. He was an advocate of the Waite school of the Golden Dawn, which is of no consequence... There are a handful of very great traditional names in the occult movement that are worthy to be categorized all by themselves. I am not in that area. Nonetheless, I consider myself more in the nature of somebody who has taken seriously the work of H.P.B., Crowley and a few of the others, and popularized them in the sense of making them somewhat more intelligible to the layman.

HYATT: Can you say more about the Golden Dawn?

REGARDIE: The Golden Dawn was founded by, and was an offshoot of, some early Masonic Rosicrucian organizations in England. That is, they were so-called Rosicrucian orders that limited their membership to high grade Masons. There isn't too much evidence to indicate they knew a very great deal about esotericism as such. At least that is one of the common criticisms; I'm not sure about that. If Mathers and Wescott and Woodman came out of the *Societas Rosicruciana* in Anglia, if they came out of that, they were pretty well informed, so I think it would be fallacious to assume that they were merely masonic dilettantes as claimed by the arch-heretic critic, Ellic Howe. What it stood for, was what similar organizations throughout the ages have stood for, the teaching of a form of esotericism which expressed the spirit of the age. Now by esotericism we mean a form of teaching which can be found in every clime, in every country, in every religion, as when Jesus said to his disciples, "to the multitude I speak in parables, to you I speak in plain ordinary language." Well the ordinary language was the esotericism, and the parables are the nonsense that the lay folk accept about religion or philosophy and all the occult sciences. The Golden Dawn, in some manner, managed to obtain access to various phases of the occult arts, some of which have been known earlier, in fact many of them can be found in the British Museum. But, even so, Mathers and Westcott gave them a new twist that made them more intelligible and more readily grasped by the modern man. Apart from that, however, there was a very great deal of teaching that didn't come from the British Museum, that didn't come from ancient manuscripts, that in some manner which I don't purport to understand, or wish to explain at the moment, they had access to great quantities of teaching that was unique to the Golden Dawn. For example, the Enochian System, so-called, was known before, in very rudimentary form. But as Dr. Head once pointed out, Dee and Kelley obtained a great deal of material, but they hadn't the faintest idea how to use it. Under the stimulus of the genius of the Golden Dawn, primarily Mathers, this was transformed into an encyclopedic synthesis that included every minute portion of the current Golden Dawn teaching, and was made into a workable systematic whole.

HYATT: What is the practical purpose of the Golden Dawn?

REGARDIE: What is the practical purpose of so many modern systems? That is to render a person whole. To give them more insight into their meaning, into their significance, into their functions as human beings, this is their goal. Where they came from, where they are now, and whither they are going. It's a method of developing a whole person, who is aware of all the hidden facets of his whole nature and knows how to bring them into play at will.

HYATT: It seems to be a very lofty goal. How does the Golden Dawn attempt to accomplish this?

REGARDIE: It attempts to accomplish this by certain exercises, by meditations and by ritual. All three of them were combined together in a very skillful manner, so that the student who really was, let us say, a person capable of initiating his own progress, of being a self-starter, would be able to take this vast body of knowledge and apply it to himself and thus, to use one of the phrases in the Adeptus Minor Grade, to gradually unite himself to his essential divinity and thus become more than human.

HYATT: You've mentioned over the years that you've experienced disappointment in some people who have been attracted to the Golden Dawn and to the occult in general, and have made some prescriptions that are available to the general public to remedy this problem. Can you clarify this point?

REGARDIE: All right, yes. I'll get myself in trouble again. (Laughter) Many of them are dilettantes, many of them are somewhat unbalanced people, and many of them are highly neurotic people. Some of them are just plain escapists, using occultism and magic as means of escaping from their own personal, emotional and neurotic problems. This is not the function of the Golden Dawn, or any other legitimate occult system. I'm critical of many of them, not merely of the dilettantes that I've just called attention to, but even of the better names, like Crowley, for whom I've enormous admiration at the same time. I've put that on record in many places and I regard him as one of the great figures in the history of occultism. But nonetheless, for example, when he published the Golden Dawn material, either he or his editors (which included some great names), somehow botched up the whole editing job. In Equinox 2 and 3 a great deal of the Golden Dawn teaching was given, but it was so doctored and so distorted, that if that were left there without recourse to any other body of knowledge, it would seem most inadequate. Crowley's genius was so great, that while he understood the Golden Dawn System well, he had very little ability to bring it down to the level of the layman with whom he was going to deal. He wasn't going to spend his life with geniuses of this kind, because there are too few of those around. So he was going to have to begin with little people, silly people. But, he had no patience with them, and, he had very little ability to bring down this vast body of knowledge to their level. I have to admit, without patting myself on the back, that I am one of the little people who had the ability to take some of this profound teaching, to succeed where Crowley failed in making it a coherent body of knowledge, to bring it to the level of, let's say, the man of average intelligence. Not so that he who runs may read, but that he who stands still and studies would be able to discern it in a coherent useful body of knowledge that might enable him to transcend the ordinary limitation of the unenlightened human state and achieve a higher so-called cosmic consciousness.

HYATT: It is said by some that organizations like the Golden Dawn have at their bag a form of elitism.

REGARDIE: I will accept that totally. I would say that The Golden Dawn is an elitist system. Even in its heyday during the late 90s and in the early part of this century, there probably were never more than 250 people at most in all the manifold temples in England. And yet, those 250 people, and that body of knowledge, even after the rebellions that resulted in the breakup of the Order into component parts, have nonetheless leavened the whole of occultism and brought about a great dispersal of this kind of information. It is my fervent hope that as time goes on, and as this knowledge becomes more available to a greater and greater number of people, this elitism will spread. That is, it is for those few who are willing to take evolution into their own hands, and make these attempts to transform themselves. The great mass of people are quite willing to drift along. They want no part or have no idea of voluntary forms of evolution, self-induced or self-devised.

HYATT: How would you differentiate elitism from sweet and light occultism?

REGARDIE: Let's go with the elitist first. The elitist belongs to no particular class, no particular race and to no particular sect. They are individuals who have courage enough, insight enough, determination and persistence enough, to take life into their own hands to proceed with the job of dealing with the reality of themselves, good, bad or indifferent, and attempt to wield themselves into a coherent whole. The "sweet and lighters," to use a name coined by one modern teacher—are metafizzlers. They are metaphysical people who see only good, and sweetness and light; nothing else exists for them. There is no evil in the world, there are no bad people, there are only good people gone a little bit sour, but all is light and sweet. The realists and elitists, the Golden Dawn Adepts, if you like, have no such delusions.

HYATT: So the Golden Dawn Adept, ideally, would be a person who would be willing and able to face all components of his own personality, without either ignoring them, repressing them or denying them. The "sweet and light" people simply ignore anything that doesn't fit in with their preconceived ideas or wishes.

REGARDIE: Right. In the Golden Dawn, in the rituals of Practicus or the Philosophus grade, there is a nice phrase extrapolated from the Chaldean Oracles, so-called, in which it says, "Nature teaches us, and the oracles also affirm, that even the evil germs of matter may alike be made useful and good." In other words, there is nothing in man, absolutely nothing, which cannot be used in order to further the Great Work, to further his own psycho-spiritual development into an integrated, illuminated human being. There were several passages in some of the rituals and in some of the documents of the Golden Dawn, which speak of the "evil persona," the Qlippoth, the so-called evil elements of man. When mastered and put in their proper place, they may serve him as a mighty steed, a powerful beast whereupon he may ride to wherever he wants to go.

HYATT: That viewpoint sounds very similar to Jung's and Reich's ideas.

REGARDIE: Exactly. There is little difference. The rejected elements are always latent and when given enough provocation and stimulus will always rise up to haunt the individual when he least expects it. Therefore they have to be faced, dealt with, and incorporated into the very heart of one's being.

HYATT: You make the point over and over again that it is your desire, in fact your demand, that any person desiring to be a neophyte and take his place in the Golden Dawn, go through some form of intensive therapy which will help him realize some of these shadowy factors and integrate them into his personality, so as not to be overwhelmed by the immense forces that are released through the Golden Dawn teachings and practices. From what you have mentioned to me privately from time to time, this is not happening. This must be a great disappointment to you.

REGARDIE: It is a tremendous disappointment. In fact, something has happened in recent years over which I feel rather betrayed. One person to whom I spoke some years ago, and who attempted to form a new Golden Dawn Temple, swore to me by all that was good and holy, that this would be one of the basic rules that would be insisted upon—that any incoming member of the Order would be required to engage in some form of psychotherapy. And we agreed on ANY form; it didn't make any difference whether it was Jungian, Freudian, Reichian, Adlerian, Eclectic or what, as long as they had enough psychotherapy of any kind to make them aware of this vast area which can be colloquially called the unconscious. Parts of themselves which they do not know, and have not known, but which have to be brought into purview of the whole self and incorporated into the total self. As time went on, this person intoxicated by the apparent growth of the Temple, dropped this proviso that we both had agreed upon, and which was one of the factors that I insisted on if I was to give any help. As a result, all sorts of squabbles have recently overtaken the temple, over which I wash my hands altogether. Recently, as a result of these squabbles, I am informed by the Hierophant that it has been decided, therefore, to reinstate the original rule, to insist that all newcoming members between the grade of Neophyte and Adeptus Minor have at least a minimum of 100 hours of any form of psychotherapy. I feel a great deal better about the 100 hours; it's still nowhere near enough, but the hope that I have secretly, is that by the time they've had 100 hours of psychotherapy they will realize the enormous need they have for further depth psychotherapy in order to prepare them for the great stresses and strains that the Great Work imposes on the organism. They will be willing to go further, and therefore follow it through to the end, thus incorporating the experience of psychotherapy into the experience of the Great Work. In other words, one is part of the other. Psychotherapy is the preparation, and the Great Work, the magical procedure of the Golden Dawn, call it whatever name you will, is the fulfillment of the promise that is revealed by, let's say, the preliminary hours and years of psychotherapy.

HYATT: Some people would say that you are pretty tough in your demands for gaining this knowledge and insight. They might feel that all is really necessary is their love for the Great Work and their intellectual commitment.

REGARDIE: Sincerity, intellect and love are nowhere near enough. Nowhere near enough. It reminds me of the title of a book by a prominent psychoanalyst in recent years, *Love Is Not Enough.* Love is *not* enough in the Great Work. The history of the Golden Dawn is replete with people who had love, devotion, intellect and all the other so-called great virtues, but nonetheless nothing came of their efforts. The Order went down to oblivion. The Order was torn asunder by strife, warfare, by internecine conflicts, by rebellions. A great deal of that *might,* and I use that word advisedly, might have been obviated by most of the members taking psychotherapy. Now I say *might,* admittedly, because we know that even in the very psychoanalytic organizations, even though the members did have psychoanalysis, psychotherapy in one form or another, they were still split at times by personality squabbles, by differences of opinion. However these organizations exist in full force today. They have not gone down to oblivion, like the Golden Dawn did. Only now is there a hope for its complete resurrection. But let's say that it is one form of psychic insurance that there will be less turmoil and destruction than might otherwise be the case.

HYATT: Some people in the occult field are very critical about the use of what are known as psychedelic drugs. What is your feeling about this?

REGARDIE: I'd have to remark first of all, that the Golden Dawn, *per* se, never approved of the use of psychedelics or any drugs. That's only one part of the story. The other part of the story is that throughout history, as far back as we can go, we know there is evidence, that many of the gurus in India, Tibet, Israel, and other parts of the world, relied on the use of psychedelics for many purposes. Crowley probably had the wisest and sanest approach to this whole problem, and that was that the beginner in the Great Work only has vague hopes of achieving certain psycho-spiritual states; he has no direct knowledge of them. Therefore, with the judicious use of some of these drugs he might be given a foretaste of where he is going, and what he is working for. Once he tasted that, once having experienced that, he might be willing to make the expenditure of time and effort in following the other exercises and disciplines that would help him to get to where he wants to go without the aid of drugs.

HYATT: Some people who I have talked to over the years have said that there is no need for psychotherapy, no need for the Golden Dawn, no need for self-work. They firmly believe that the simple use of these substances would be more than sufficient to bring a person to their higher and divine self.

REGARDIE: Totally untrue, as I know you would agree from your own observations. I don't think there is any evidence to support and warrant that. The drugs produce a state which is akin and analogous to some of the mystical states. But as the drug wears off, so does the state wear off, and there is very little recollection and very little endurance of the psychedelic state. So therefore, that idea really doesn't hold water. The combination of the use of the psychedelics AND the various disciplines, train the mind, train the psyche, train the organism of the student or the practitioner, to retain within his consciousness, within his organism not merely consciousness *per se,* but to retain the memory of the spiritual state he has experienced, and therefore enable him AT WILL to return to that state whenever he so desires.

HYATT: To change topics on you quickly, what are the mysterious Rosicrucians? Are they similar to the Secret Chiefs? (Laughter)

REGARDIE: They were not ever spoken of as Secret Chiefs. It was a group of unknown people who were quite evidently Christians, Christian mystics, who had apparently become aware of the mystical traditions which predated their Lord by aeons. By the way, one of the legends states that one of them, the very father of the Order, Christian Rosenkreutz, had been brought up in a Catholic monastery, and at an early age had traveled all over Europe and the middle East and North Africa, where he had been initiated into the Qabalah, alchemy and magic, etc. and brought it back to Europe, to his native monastery. There he initiated three or four of his brethren and thus began the Rosicrucian Order. Some critics are inclined to say that is mythology. Be that as it may, and it may well be mythology, but by the end of the 17th century, there were small bodies of people which had sprung up using the three Rosicrucian classics as the basis for their fraternity and were teaching the Qabalah, magic and alchemy, obviously in a very secret way.

The Protestant and Catholic churches would have made very short work of them if they had come out in the open with that kind of knowledge. But they were attracting bodies of people to them, or small groups of people and setting up organizations which used the word Rosicrucian in one way or another. Some of them infiltrated the Masonic Order which had its origin around the same time, the early part of the 18th century. In fact there was a degree in one of the rites, the Scottish Rite, which is called the Rose Croix degree. This may imply that some of the Rosicrucian bodies had made a link with the Masons as a means of perpetuating their knowledge. This is one theory. The other theory is that the Jesuits who were intent on destroying the Rosicrucians and the Masons had set up phony degrees as a means of bringing discredit to this Rosicrucian movement.

HYATT: I noticed when I said "Secret Chiefs" you laughed a bit.

REGARDIE: I laugh…it's a difficult subject to handle. First of all I don't like dealing overtly with the topic of Secret Chiefs because the whole thing has been so abused by idiotic people that almost to talk about them means reducing oneself to their superstitious and psychotic level.

HYATT: This is a good chance to make YOUR point about this problem public. People do walk around saying "the Secret Chiefs said this or that."

REGARDIE: Of course they do. They are idiots or worse. That's why I dislike talking about it except to say that most of the people who do talk about it are talking out of their hats. However, where there is smoke, there is some little fire. And I am willing to admit that there may be some few beings in the flesh, as human beings, who live here and there, without our being aware of them, who have "super-normal power" and "super-normal knowledge" that enable them to direct the destinies of organizations like the Golden Dawn or other movements. But there is no point in going hunting for them because if they are Secret Chiefs they are going to remain Secret Chiefs and you'd be much wiser leaving the whole topic alone. If they want you they will come looking for you. You don't have to go looking for them. It's like in the theatrical business, the agent says, "Don't ring me, I'll ring you." So the point is, don't bother looking for the Secret Chiefs. If you are going to be of any importance to the Great Work, to the Golden Dawn or any similar organizations, if you have the potentiality of being useful they will somehow look you up. All your searching in the world is never going to help you find them, never. So leave them alone and go about doing your business whatever that may be, meditation, ritual magic, or all the other allied facets of the Great Work, go ahead and do that and develop your own self to the best of your ability, then maybe one of these days if all goes well, and if you can be useful to the Great Work, one of them may come along and say "Look here, buster, you've got some more work to do and we'll help you." Even if something like that did happen I would advise that your ego be in its proper place.

HYATT: That is a great explanation. How do you differentiate the Western Esoteric tradition from the Eastern Esoteric tradition?

REGARDIE: In reality there isn't a great deal of difference. The difference is largely one of terminology. For example, I have toyed with the idea of making a comparison of Mahayana Buddhism and the Tibetan system with the Golden Dawn. They are very similar. There isn't that much difference. So far as the Hindu systems are concerned, they are more sweet and light than the Western and the Tibetan systems. The Tibetan systems are very much like the Western systems to me. They're tough-minded and they don't encourage the sweet and light love tripe that is characteristic of the Hindu system. The Tibetan systems and the Western are very similar. The Hindus stress more than sweet and light. They're more loving, and at the same time much more ego-expansive in that they identify themselves with God after certain experiences, and so forth, which in the West is done with a great deal more caution.

HYATT: You seem to have little trust or respect for organizations and groups who are promoting love as the basis of their system and the cure-all for everything.

REGARDIE: I have very little trust for them. Which is not to say that I don't think love in that sense of the word is terribly important. But I don't like the tossing around of the word LOVE, I don't like this kind of sloppy sentimentality. It usually usurps every other kind of real work. They merely sit around and talk. God loves you, Jesus loves you, Buddha loves you...they do very little work and nothing is accomplished.

HYATT: So in a certain sense you could be considered another western master of work as some people have called Crowley the great Master of work. He did not let his people sit around and talk all day about how much they love each other. Instead he demanded effort out of everything they did. Worship is work.

REGARDIE: I don't consider myself a master—in no way. Let's say I'm an advocate of work and not a master. He may be a master. I'm not. The less gab they have, the less emphasis on I love you, you love me, God loves us, and I love God, the more emphasis on facts. Look, you're a human being, and you've got a certain amount of guts—use it as a means of scaling the ladders of achieving the heights. Love and God will take care of themselves. First be yourself, damn it, and stop talking about things you have no understanding of. This is my attitude.

HYATT: That's a great statement. And even though you don't regard yourself as a master, many do. This idea about Love and Work leads me to another question. Why is there such a separation between the body and the spirit in this work? This to me seems not only false but very sad.

REGARDIE: It's very sad actually, yes. This is one of the many reasons why I insist that anybody getting into the Golden Dawn, the Great Work, MUST precede any practical work with some psychotherapy, because the experience of any form of psychotherapy will at least make the student aware that he does have a real sexuality and a rich emotional creative life which must not be bottled up, repressed or inhibited. He must always realize that repression only leads to compulsion in one form or another and interferes with the accomplishment of his goals. Therefore we must rid ourselves of both repression and compulsion. One of the best ways of accomplishing this goal is through Reichian therapy. But as I said before, any form of psychotherapy will go far towards ridding the student of his armoring, thus aiding in the acquisition of real insight which is the first step towards the emergence of spiritual understanding and illumination.

HYATT: That seems to be what the Tantra Yogis were saying as well. Tantra, of course, is concerned with "method-technique." It is not simply concerned with sex as is commonly thought. It seems that Tantra posits the view that the power and force of the sex instinct can be used to make something happen—maybe a peak experience or enlightenment. They approach the whole idea of sex differently, very differently from the Semitic religions and Hinduism. Western religions are always worried about sex—it is an obsession with them. There are always co-conditions for partaking of pleasure—marriage, love, children—always conditions. Why do you think such a split has occurred between sex and spirit?

REGARDIE: That's really a very complex thing, and is not readily answered. Suffice it to say that it has developed and it's dangerous, very dangerous. It doesn't intrinsically belong to the Great Work. In the Great Work every phase of one's makeup has to be used, employed and integrated to make a whole. Nothing can be denied. Nothing. To exclude one's sexuality is really to ask for a very great deal of trouble in the development of neurotic and even psychotic traits. In modern times, the only thing I can assume is that some of the exponents of the system had neurotic problems of their own. However much I admire H.P.B., and I've put myself on record on this and I will stand by it, I have the greatest admiration for the old girl, but nonetheless, she was brought up as a Christian, as a member of the Eastern Orthodox Church and she's inherited all the worst aspects of Christian inhibition where sexuality is concerned.

Whatever the Indian influences she encountered over the years merely strengthened her negative attitudes towards sexuality.

HYATT: There is almost the same thing about money and the Great Work.

REGARDIE: Yes. It's almost as if most hold the Christian point of view. It is all a bunch of nonsense. One of the motivations of this, I think, and Mathers has expressed this somehow in one of the Golden Dawn writings, is that one may get too caught up in self-indulgence that he fancies money will bring. You can do whatever you want to, get anything you want to with money, and therefore become a little bit lax in one's devotion to the Great Work. It's a damn poor argument actually, because the same thing is true of poverty. You can get so attached to poverty that you groan and grunt about it and then begin to use all sorts of excuses, "I don't do this and I can't do that, because at the moment I'm too poor to have a gown, I'm too poor to have a room where I can meditate, I'm too poor to have a temple, etc."

HYATT: As one of the great gurus said, a man with no clothes who sits under a tree and meditates, can and often does, become attached to his place under the tree. So in that sense what you are saying is that it is not the problem with materiality, money, sex, or ego *per se,* it is the blind attachment to anything which creates the problem.

REGARDIE: It's the person himself who is the problem. He stands in his own way. And again I insist that this is why some form of psychotherapy is needed... To get rid of these neurotic attachments or fixations to sex, to money, to the parents, to the ego, or whatever. Nothing really happens until this is done.

HYATT: As we know there has been a growing hatred of the occult movement by the born-again Christians. It almost seems that where the cross goes, so goes the sword. What do you feel about their fanaticism and their potential for violence?

REGARDIE: I find this is characteristic of all the Semitic religions, Judaism, Christianity and Mohammedanism, have always been spread by the sword. They are the great scourge on the escutcheon of the West. For example, when one reads in the Bible about the entry of the primitive tribes of Israel led by Moses and Joshua and the Kings into the land of Canaan, it was always with the sword. They went in and wiped out thousands of people in the name of Jehovah and took over the land. Then along come the Christians who did exactly the same thing. They were thoroughgoing barbarians, and spread the cross with the sword. Some of the most awful crimes against mankind were committed during the Crusades. That makes gruesome reading. Another set of gruesome reading materials is to be found in the conquest of the Americas—Mexico, Peru, etc., where the friar, the monk, went hand in hand with the soldiers to convert with the sword and with the garrote. The same thing is going on today. If the born-agains, if the Christians, had their way, they would suppress every particular poisonous brand. So Christianity hasn't changed much in the last 2,000 years, the cross and the sword still going together. In fact one of the most popular Christian hymns is "Onward Christian Soldiers... Marching on to war with the cross of Jesus, etc..."

HYATT: Do you feel that they are going to gain more power as time goes on?

REGARDIE: Yes, I do feel that they are going to gain more power in the next 50 to 100 years, but I have the intuition, or the optimistic feeling, that this nonetheless is the last dying gasp, or the last gasp of a dying religion. The day of Christianity is relatively over. They seem to be more powerful at the moment, and in many ways they are, but there is also a riptide, a backlash, going on which is also highly antagonistic to their activities. There is going to be a fearful clash in the near future which will result, I think, in the total elimination of Christianity altogether. There is the rise of the Oriental religions. The Moslems are no longer taking things sitting down and letting the Christians walk all over them. They are becoming more militant, which I say is fine for the moment. Let them become more militant, and let the Christians become more militant. They may wipe each other out to leave the world safe for those who want to go their own way in the search for truth.

HYATT: The Christians would regard, I guess, The Golden Dawn and its teachings as black magic or...devil worship. (Laughter)

REGARDIE: And heretical and so on and on. Ha!

HYATT: Why do you think they would say that about us? (Laughter)

REGARDIE: Let's say when the Rosicrucians began in the early part of the 17th century, the Christian Church and the Jesuits thought any deviation from the dogma laid down by the Church was heretical and should be investigated by the Inquisition. The victims were given over to the stake.

HYATT: So can we posit that the born-again Christians are becoming another form of inquisition?

REGARDIE: They are indeed. Indeed. I fear it's very, very dangerous. We won't mention any names, but there is a very prominent preacher on T.V. who I'm sure would love to institute an Inquisition and get rid of all those who don't follow his particular brand of insanity.

HYATT: I wonder who that could be? (Laughter) Robert Anton Wilson mentioned his name in his book *Prometheus Rising* for which you wrote an introduction. Bob is very optimistic about the coming age, *The New Age,* as he sees it, and he is very optimistic about the effects of technology and life extension, etc. I know that in many ways you agree with him and you feel very happy that there is this feeling in the air, but at the same time you have some strong doubts about this.

REGARDIE: I am in almost total agreement with him, but I have the gravest doubts that it is going to occur in the immediate future. He believes before the year 2000 we will have space colonies, and that Christianity will no longer be as vociferous as it is, and that we will be entering the New Age. I don't feel quite so optimistic. It is too utopian. And I don't trust utopias. I think it's going to take some hundreds of years before we really get rid of the pernicious effects of the born-again Christians and Christianity as a whole. Probably a couple of hundred years. It's going to peter out slowly (no pun intended). It'll go through various retrogressions and surges of power, alternating, but eventually in a couple of hundred years it will fizzle out and then new religious forms, new religious expressions, that will be much more allied to the method of science, will come into being. But before this there will be Holy Wars. I hate to say it, but in many ways I don't have to say it.

HYATT: You have expressed concern for this civilization elsewhere in this interview and I hear this concern again. Can you say more?

REGARDIE: Yes I am, but we needn't feel too badly about that...civilizations have risen, come to maturity, and then died. That's an old but true story of all things. Everything has its origin, birth, maturity, and death. Cultures are no different. America, which I love, is no different. The way the Christian culture in the last 2,000 years has dealt with the world is nothing to make a very great fuss about. It is apparent that the time is coming when it's going down to destruction. If my memory serves me right, over a hundred years ago, H.P.B. wrote somewhere in *The Secret Doctrine* that western civilization is coming to an end. How soon, she didn't know, but she certainly said within the next century. Apparently one of her predictions is about to come to pass. Whether it does or not (although I fancy that it will), I want to see the Great Work (The Golden Dawn and other worthy systems) preserved in another part of the world, so that students there will have the wherewithal to continue their Way if anything disastrous does happen.

HYATT: Falcon Press has published *The Eye in the Triangle: An Interpretation of Aleister Crowley,* and *The Legend of Aleister Crowley.* Sales are good and we are pleased. However we are unhappy that so many serious occult students fear or hate Crowley. Can you provide any insights into this unfortunate phenomenon.

REGARDIE: I don't know that any of my insights are new, but I think a great deal of that was due to his own ego. He had a colossal ego. He was almost like the Ford Company—

every knock is a boost. (Laughter) So he didn't mind having himself damned, so long as it was done publicly, and that it gave him notoriety, giving the world notice that he was around. He kept all his foibles, however many there were, always brought to the forefront so that the world was aware of Aleister Crowley and his pranks. If he committed adultery, which one or two people still do today, he made a point of insuring that everybody knew about it. And, if on occasion, he indulged in homosexuality, he publicized that, too. If he took drugs, he made sure that everybody knew about that also. Moreover he fabricated all sorts of lovely stories to blacken his reputation further; that he sacrificed children and killed women. All that is a lot of poppycock. It gave him notoriety. He was having a wonderful time, having a good laugh at the expense of the general public. What he didn't realize, and this shows that despite his genius what a damn fool he was, there were journalists and writers who took him seriously, and really condemned him for this sort of thing. And actually lived off him. They made a lot of money off him. Some of them even took seriously his statement that he killed male children, 150 of them a year. Obviously, if they had read the footnote involved, they would have realized that he was speaking in terms of symbolism, and that he was having intercourse 150 times a year. And that was all there was to it. But some of these people licked their chops and thought this was a rotten, dirty old man.

He made good copy, so they really lambasted him. Thus a great deal of his bad reputation, despite everything else creative that he did, has to be laid to his own door. I have very little sympathy really with what he did, because if he wanted to leave his mark on mankind without these black marks against him, he could have done it very easily. But his ego ran away with him, and he thought he was having a wonderful lark, not taking time out to consider that everybody didn't have the same kind of humor that he did. They took all his jokes seriously and now they are coming home to roost. One reviewer in the *Los Angeles Times* many years ago, in reviewing Crowley's autobiography says, "Crowley was a Victorian hippy." Be that as it may, Victorian hippies are no different from modern hippies. They don't go around killing 150 babies a year and publicizing it and not winding up in jail. Crowley was an idiot insofar as he did that. Now he had his own rationalizations for that, and most of them were that he was intent on destroying the old set of morals and the old set of clichés about human behavior, so therefore what he did should be made public so as to get rid of the guilts that were attached to sex, etc. Apparently it didn't work out that way.

HYATT: Some people say that Crowley, if he were alive today, would look quite normal in Los Angeles, or San Francisco or New York.

REGARDIE: Oh, there's no question about that. He'd be just one of thousands and maybe millions. EXCEPT, of course, his genius would still make him stand out more vigorously.

HYATT: But in terms of his homosexuality?

REGARDIE: ...in San Francisco it would not be noticed. But his genius would still shine very brightly.

HYATT: In 1984 Falcon published Crowley's *The World's Tragedy.* You wrote an introduction to this book, and you considered it to be very iconoclastic.

REGARDIE: There were two things that stamped that book as iconoclastic, and gave it a very small distribution in 1910, when it was first published. First, it was very anti-Christian, and the second, he overtly advertised the fact that he was a homosexual, that he was a sodomite, and that the book, therefore, was not to be sold in England. It might be sold anywhere else, but not in England. It might be sold anywhere else, but not in England, or he would have wound up in jail, since sodomy was against the law. His attack on Christianity was really a lampoon. It's very, very funny, and it's very blasphemous, and very eloquent, and I'm sure most of the good Christians today would find it very, very offensive. They found it offensive in 1910, and despite the amount of anti-Christian books that have been written in the last 60 to 70 years, it would still strike a number of Christians as very painful to their very, very delicate nerves. But it was a combination of those two things, his avowed homosexuality, and his total and complete contempt and hatred of Christianity, which earned that book a reputation which prevented it from being published again.

HYATT: Some people have said you were in love with four "things" in your life...

REGARDIE: Wine, women and song. (Laughter)

HYATT: That's only three. (Laughter) But how do you see now these four loves of yours? (H.P.B., Crowley, The Golden Dawn and Reich.)

REGARDIE: Yes, I would say that, Yes. I would say that Blavatsky was my first love. I say that she has influenced me more profoundly than almost any other occultist. I use the word occultist truly in her case, rather than occult writers. I first read her when I was about 16, and studied her for years, and occasionally still study her. I can still open up *The Secret Doctrine* with a great deal of curiosity, and before too long find myself really involved and engrossed, and can read for a couple of hours, finding it even more illuminating than I did 60 years ago. From her, of course I ventured afield into areas indicated by her and discovered Crowley. With him, of course, my contact was much more personal than it was with H.P.B. That's because I never knew her; she died around 1890, and of course, I wasn't born for another 17 years. But Crowley was alive when I was still a young man, and without going into a number of details, I met him to become his secretary for some few years, and had a good deal of contact with him. From him I learned a very, very great deal. What I learned from him is very difficult to put into words. I don't think I learned a great deal of magic from him; I did learn a great deal of magic from his writings. *The Equinox* especially. I soaked myself in the volumes of *The Equinox* for years, and knew them backwards and forwards, inside out, etc. Crowley somehow had an enormous maturing effect on me. I was a young boy when I met him, I had just turned 20. Somehow, in his own inimitable way, he helped me to grow up and become something of an adult. I owe him a very, very great deal, a very great deal. Later we fell out, which was due to my own stupidity. After I recovered from my annoyance of a quarrel with him, I reestablished my admiration for him, and my love, if you like, and still hold him in the highest esteem, although I am a great deal more objective about him now that I ever was before. So that accounts for Blavatsky and Crowley. Then there is Wilhelm Reich. I discovered him around 1947. Again we don't need to go into the how and why. I became enamored of him almost immediately. Within a very short period of time got myself involved in Reichian therapy, in which I stayed for four years. Reich and I had a number of personal communications, which must remain private. I explain why in my book on Reich to be published in 1984. Lastly there is the Golden Dawn. In 1932 Crowley went off to Europe to show his paintings in Berlin, where subsequently they were destroyed by the Nazis. Anyway, he was gone for several years, and I was left at loose ends. At that time I became secretary to Thomas Burke just to keep me going. In that time I started my first literary work. I wrote two books, *The Garden of the Pomegranates,* an outline of the Qabalah, which wasn't too good; it was a series of notes that were thrown together. That was followed by *The Tree of Life* which Riders commissioned me to write. I told them what I had in mind, and they gave me £50, that was $250, which to me in those days was a great deal of money. In three or four months, I turned out *The Tree of Life* which, though a good book, languished for a long while. A copy of it came to the attention of The Golden Dawn people through the medium of Dion Fortune. Much to my surprise, one of the chiefs of The Golden Dawn in Bristol came to visit me, and to my further astonishment, invited me to join. One of them had had a vision that a young man with an important book would join the Order. So they identified that with me and *The Tree of Life* and since I was at a loose end, Crowley being gone, etc. etc., I accepted it. And that was one of the wisest moves that I have ever made in my life. It was there, then, that much of my magical knowledge and experience came to fruition, and were organized. For awhile I had a teacher in the form of the Golden Dawn chiefs who lavished a good deal of care and training on me, etc., etc. I am grateful to them... Very! That was a very important part of my life... It is impossible to say which is more important. All of them were, in their own ways and probably, of the four, Crowley and The Golden Dawn were the most valuable. They have left indelible marks on my life, and my career if I want to use that term, but certainly on my personal life. Crowley first, and The Golden Dawn second. On the other hand, I cannot separate Crowley from The Golden Dawn, because Crowley was The Golden Dawn, and The Golden Dawn was Crowley. Crowley was, to use one of my earlier clichés, a graduate without honor from the

Golden Dawn. He took the Golden Dawn teaching and transformed some of it, used other bits of it literally, but still it was all based on The Golden Dawn, even though he gave his Order another name, the A∴A∴. So I felt very much at home in The Golden Dawn, and really had no problem absorbing the material, sailing through it very, very rapidly just as Crowley had many years earlier.

HYATT: Now you're a few days from being 78, you've seen a lot of things, you've done a lot of things. What are your present interests and what would you like to do?

REGARDIE: Wine, women and song. (Laughter) Gosh, that sure sounds like Crowley, doesn't it? It's true I love good wine, beautiful women, and good music more than I ever did before! My other interests (laughter) in life are the same as they've been for the last 60 years. In other words, I am devoted and dedicated to the Great Work and I want to see it spread. I want to see The Golden Dawn renewed, reformed, started by young, vigorous, alive people with a system made much more rigid and elite in the sense of deliberately imposed discipline, with psychotherapy made an intrinsic part of the program. Teaching some of different, nonetheless it still fits in with the general framework as being an account of a simplified magical system with all the depth left out and simply relying upon a kind of auto-suggestion, if you like. Like the ritual of Thoth, which really consists of auto-suggestive and mnemonic phrases which are in better English than most of the Christian Science affirmations, but still consist of the same sort of thing. Yoga, particularly hatha yoga and a few others, is not much different in essence from my interest in Reich and relaxation techniques. Or rather Yoga is an elaborate extension of Reich. So later when I discovered Reich and his breathing techniques, it wasn't really that new to me. It was already part and parcel of the yoga system which I'd almost grown up in many, many years earlier. The only thing that was new was Reich's point of view, the whole idea of the muscular armor, the character armor, but then there was nothing really tremendously new about that either, because that was an outcropping of Freud, the superego, etc., etc. It all fits together whether anyone likes it or not. The Reichians won't like what I say, nor will some of the yogis, but there it is. I have never been a true believer of any *one* thing. I take what's best for me and leave the rest behind. This is one reason I make people mad. It's hard to box me in as a pure anything. I use all and everything.

HYATT: If you were to sum up life in one sentence, what would you say?

REGARDIE: It's a weird bloody business! I have no other cliché for life. Life is a pain at times, getting old is a pain, but I accept that. I only feel that old YHVH must have been drunk when he created this mess. Many things are arse backwards. Many are simply funny. But I firmly believe that you must have a sense of humor about the whole business, particularly if you get into this sort of work. Most people in the occult have no sense of humor. This is so important, as you try to show in your own book, *Undoing Yourself With Energized Meditation.* I know most people won't understand it. It's too complex, it's not a thing that someone can cling to. You don't let your reader rest. You're always throwing things at him. You're showing him so much. I still hold that someday it will be a classic in the field, but most people are too scared, too rigid to live through that book. Life is life, and from the occult point of view, we somehow pay off some old debts and incur some new ones, and develop ourselves as best we can, gradually and ultimately achieving the Great Work. Not in this lifetime, but perhaps in some other, and so it goes. Enlightenment and freedom are the goals.

HYATT: Thanks for the compliment, we will have to see. But if you were to choose what form you would come back in next time, in terms of reincarnation, what would you choose?

REGARDIE: I have mentioned this to you in private. What I would like, is to come back to a decent family where I would be given a good classical education first of all. And in the second place I would like to come back into a family where they were familiar with the whole series of concepts of occultism, the Great Work, the Golden Dawn. It would be rather nice to be born into a family where the Golden Dawn would be intrinsic to their point of view, to be able to pick up almost immediately where I had left off before.

HYATT: You also said, that you might like to be a Siamese pussycat.

REGARDIE: (Laughter) Well, that's a possible alternative! No, I'd still like to go on as I've been going on obviously for some time and that is to continue the Great Work until I become a Rajneesh. (Laughter)

HYATT: You don't want to become like Rajneesh!

REGARDIE: No. (Laughter) Just one of the Secret Chiefs. (sic!)

HYATT: Falcon hopes to be bringing out a couple of articles of yours next year. One of them is on Eugenics.

REGARDIE: Occult Eugenics?

HYATT: Can you expand on that?

REGARDIE: Occult Eugenics was really inspired by Crowley's silly novel *Moonchild.* That was such a gag, and such a burlesque, that it annoyed me. And he was so cruel in that book to everybody he knew that I wiped all that out from my mind and gradually over a period of years, an idea occurred to me predicated on this: that if a couple wanted to, let's say, bring into the world children who had "greater capabilities" they could use some of the magical techniques as a means of insuring that they would produce "better" children.

HYATT: I know we're jumping the gun, but can you discuss some of these techniques.

REGARDIE: Magical techniques! A bedroom where they're going to copulate which they purify by the pentagram ritual. Depending upon what kind of child they envisioned, do the invoking pentagrams and hexagrams of the planets and/or signs of the zodiac, write the appropriate kind of ritual rehearse that, and then while making love, recite the ritual with fervor. Do that several times and see if that affected the incoming reincarnating entity or attracted a higher grade being.

HYATT: That is a fascinating idea. Do you know anybody who's tried it?

REGARDIE: No. These ideas have had some kind of circulation. Once in a while I hear from somebody, but there are obviously a lot of people who have read of it but have never written to me, so who knows? Some of these things may have been experimented with, we know nothing about them. And I wouldn't tell if I did.

HYATT: I know one thing for sure, the born-again Christian movement wouldn't approve of Occult Eugenics. (Laughter, Regardie laughing hysterically.)

REGARDIE: (Still laughing) Oh no—no. None of what Falcon is publishing is going to be approved of by the born-agains, or in fact even by many occultists. You guys are too free—too loose—too different.

HYATT: You are aware that occasionally we are called the Evil Press—Devil worshipers and other silly things. Of course they call you worse. On occasions our lives are threatened by people who say they are going to put bombs in our cars—our homes, offices, etc.

REGARDIE: Those you have to accept as ever-present possibilities from the madmen outside. I've received shit like that all my life. I wouldn't pay too much attention to them. However, it's really a compliment.

HYATT: I'll try not to.

REGARDIE: They're mad, absolutely mad.

HYATT: I'll close with a statement by Dr. J. Marvin Spiegelman which he made about you: "...He once more reveals himself to be an outstanding, living occult magician, and the only one to combine this with the insight of the scholar, the caring of the psychotherapist, and the religious attitude of the spiritual man."

REGARDIE: I'll accept that, but I still like wine, women and song. (Laughter)

HYATT: Then a toast to the Great Work.

REGARDIE: Hear! Hear! So mote it be! (Laughter)

CHANNELED BY POPE NICK ON 3-10-1990

REGARDIE: By the way, Hyatt, my final words are:

"Let Them Fuck!"

The *WHO'S WHO* of the
WHO

A MANTRAM FOR
THE MUDDLED CLASS

"Monotheism has been the greatest danger of mankind... In Polytheism man [has] the power to create for himself new and individual eyes."

Freddie Nietzsche

"Leibnitz is alive and well in Southwest Ethiopia."

C.S. Hyatt, Zen Buddhist Priest
The New Western School (est. 1975)

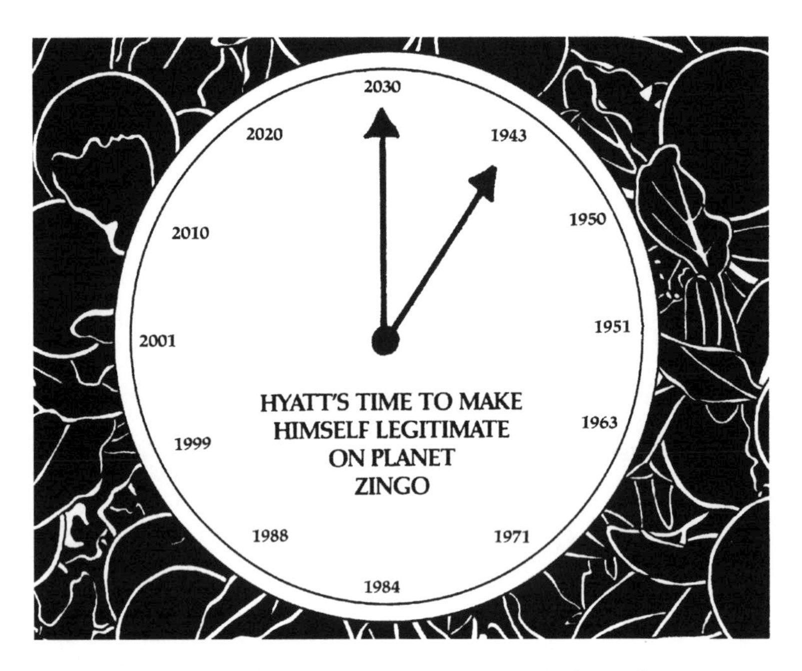

Question: Is the New Western School a "legitimate" organization?

Question: When did you become legitimate?

Answer: It's simply a function of what time zone you are in.

For the species, "monotheist legitimacy"

is a function of

how much time is left on the mortgage.

SECTION 156 – Freddie is still alive in DOGMA DAZE.

LEARY has Told it all in WHAT DOES WOMAN WANT? Has he told the truth about Hyatt?

Suffering from amnesia, Hyatt helps and hinders Leary, reminding him of all his faults and all of his virtues.

When we experience amnesia our attention has been shifted FROM something deeper which is HARDLY working US.

Have you noticed
Hyatt's amnesia techniques?

YES □

NO □

MAYBE □

I DO NOT CARE □

CULTURE IS FOR BACTERIA

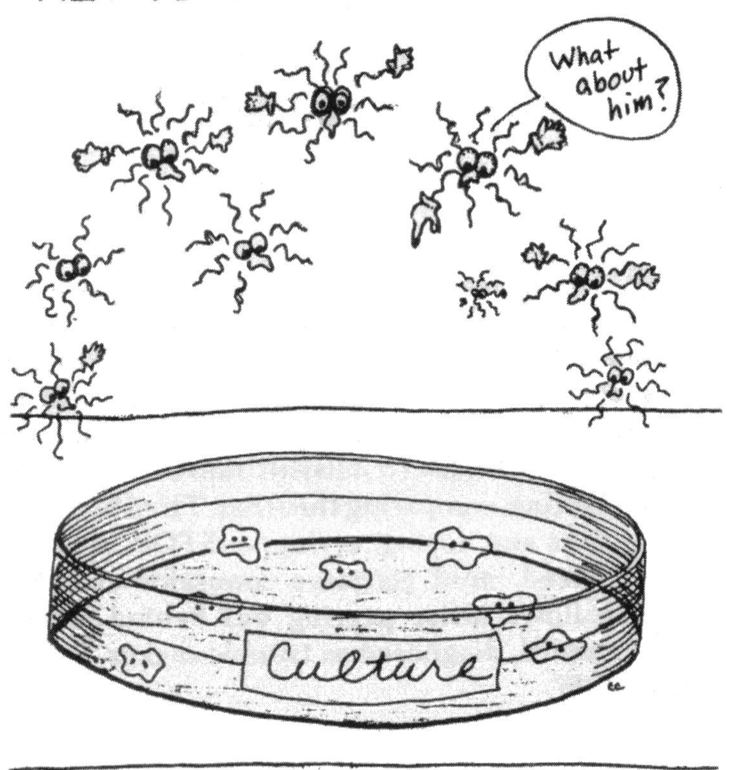

A BED TIME STORY

Powerful Monotheists setting up stakes, gallows, formally executing a time schedule for the future. Their favorite is: "It was Done Before" -- if it doesn't fit, stretch it. When all done, a shopping guide is handed out for up-coming events -- sales. Destroy anything, but don't maul the shopping. E-CON-O-CENTS, blissful housewives, dying to spend, budgeting, comparing this/that. Tired husband, muddled at day's end, trying, crying -- STOP. A phone call to girl friend, need marriage counselor executor. Hidden in gallows office peering out behind screen, husband examined, diagnosed as trouble-maker. Future looks dim NOW.

TREATMENT PLAN

Deep pile rug dressed -- all forgiven. Don't spill, walk too heavy, time for physical exam, husband suffering from exhaustion, prostate swollen, hem-i-rods bleeding. Wife needs vacation. Stretched out. Husband back worked, wife gone, mind on JOB. Got Raised.

LIGHT CIGARETTE, BINACA BLAST, TAKE A WALK

Bribe, reward, interdictions, worry, solutions, results.

Match the above 6 behaviors with the story. Ask yourself at what point did you go DEEPER.

A HAPPY TRANCE: A SUCCESS STORY

A sure sign of a MONOTHEIST is that she mostly takes Herself very seriously.

Father spent $25,000.00 -- restitution. The Wedding went perfectly -- marriage failed -- thank God No children -- Daughter OK. Picture album "living" -- good memories of things broken -- daughter drinking looks older now -- then beautiful in special dress designed -- DIVORCE successful no other like it -- a pavilion wonderful. No cash back. Son In LAW EX'ED. Father vindicated as soothsayer. Now Lawyer. His summer at New-Port, Ivy League reunions, fast ended player, faded memories -- Sunday football -- almost forgotten ——— NEW young wife -- children now that were never born -- Mexico wedding, picturesque scene, shudders open.

A VERY DEEP TRANCE

You might notice a finger flicking, a hand moving, a leg lifting, an eye twitching, an ear itching.

When you are ready you make wake deeply or lightly. There is no need to read the next line if you wish.

ALL HIGHER TRUTH IS STARING YOU IN THE FACE

A TRANCE IS NO DEEPER THAN YOU ARE

YUPPIES
THE NEW
MONOTHEISTS

In our trance of freeing ourselves to have the power, the sex and the money, we again begin to see that monomania is Monotheism.

A TRANCE IS NO DEEPER THAN YOU ARE

THE WIFE SCREAMS AT HER HUSBAND
"YOU CONTROLLING BASTARD YOU"

What this means in English is that SHE can't have his way.

A TRANCE IS NO DEEPER THAN YOU ARE

* * *

THE HUSBAND YELLS AT HIS WIFE
"YOU DIRTY BITCH YOU"

What this means in English is that HE can't have her way.

Each believes that they have a monopoly on reality. Each unfortunately is right. Each are wHIM worshippers who don't have the guts to call themselves—wHER WORSHIPPERS. Each KNOWS THE TRUTH—BUT WHO HAS THE POWER?

ANSWER: THE ONE WHO SHOWS THE LEAST FEAR.

As you might guess, we ALL are in TRANCE most of the time.

• • • • • • • • • •

We want to LEARN to say NO to TRANCES which we do not choose. To do this we will KNOW how to remember that we have FORGOTTEN.

• • • • • • • • • •

GOING DEEPER UNDER YOUR CONTROL

NO IS AN OPTION TO YES

YES IS AN OPTION TO NO

MAYBE IS AN OPTION TO BOTH

What other options do we have?
(A) Never
(B) Always
(C) Sometimes

Don't Strive

to be part of

the

Social Fabric

Strive to be

A Moth

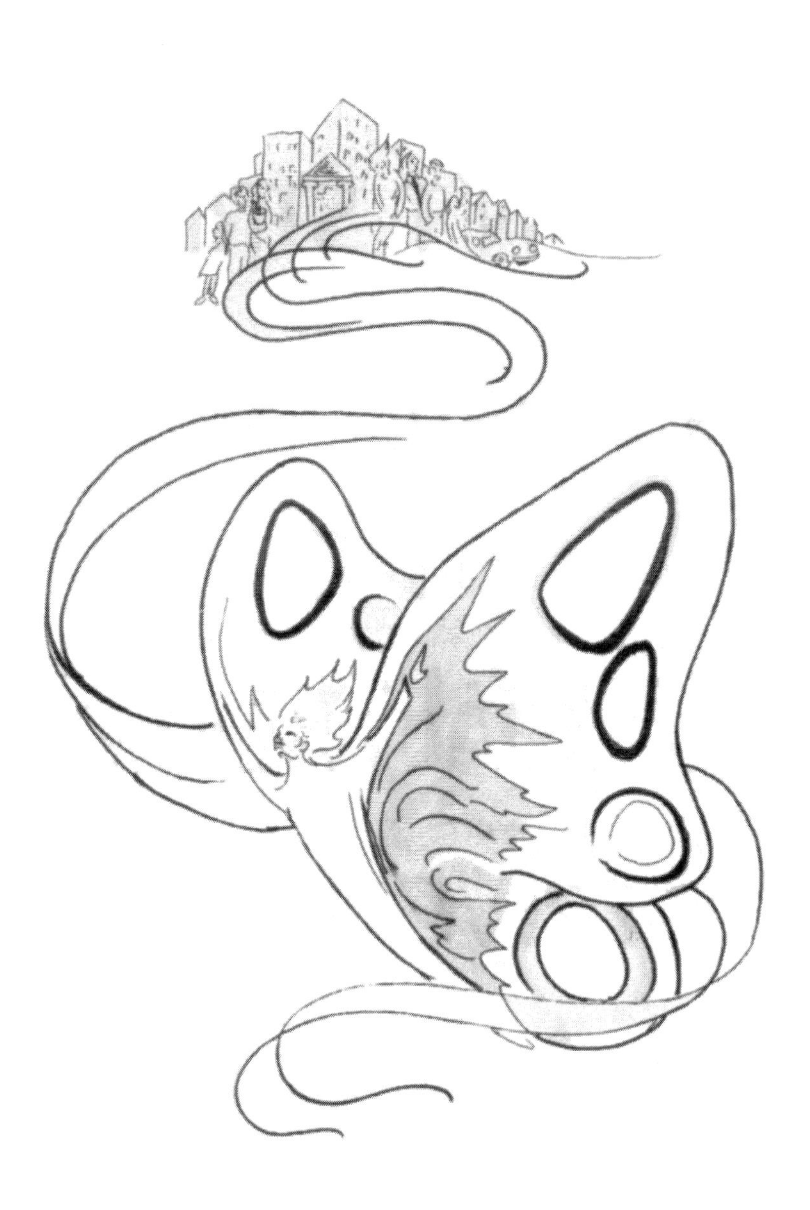

Only a monotheist can know the future?

Not remembering that self-fulfilling prophecies are self fulfilling, the monotheist creates an illusion of Order which to some degree conforms to his expectations. Using this as "proof" he insists that his definitions are inherently correct.

Not understanding this process, he attempts to MAKE the earth and its inhabitants conform to his arbitrary definitions. These are now KNOWN as morals—absolute and necessary conditions for the survival of the species. He believes that his definitions are the only way that the Will of [his] God can be served.

✧ TRANCES CONTROL THE TAKE ✧

Focusing on the MONOTHEISTIC PRINCIPLE always creates its opposite. When we see it fail, as in the case of the Christian-Altruistic Ploy, we simply create more of it by legislating LOVE, CARE and CONCERN.

In other words, are we really shooting blanks with our notions of Altruism?

Hyatt's Tripolar Formula for SUCCESS suggests that we must entertain at least two other MONO-Theistic principles, one being Hedonism, and the other being Realism.

The Tripolar Formula supports three distinct philosophies. One is Hedonism, Another is Realism and the Other is Altruism.

Most people attempt to force-fit into one of these designer genes and others AS wooden doll Sapiens. The cause of this is MONOTHEISM, the belief that diversity MUST BE reduced to a single principle: one husband, one job, one god, one home, and many children — — WARS.

"Intelligent" monotheists spend time arguing, discussing, degrading, feeling superior to other Monotheisms.

"Dumb" monotheists spend time in violent exchanges of Dogma — often dumping — pails of sweated matter.

SET — is a pre-disposition to respond to variety with singularity — — THE CURSE OF THE MONOTHEIST.

A
BLANK
PAGE
with no
#'s
TAKE A SHOT

BECAUSE BE DAMNED FOR A DOG

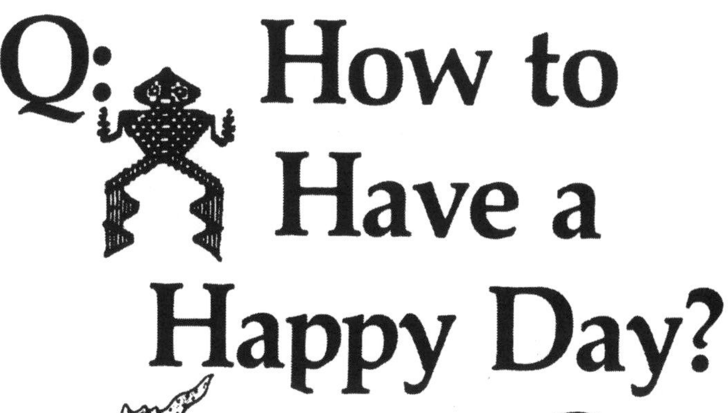

Q: How to Have a Happy Day?

A: Fire Your Lawyers & Accountants

"NO GOOD DEED GOES UNPUNISHED."

F.I. Regardie to Hyatt in a state of rage
over nosy and greedy relatives (1983)

P.S. Regardie was an optimist

"NO DEED GOES UNPUNISHED."

Pope Nick to Hyatt in a state of California
over nosy and greedy civil servants (1988)

The PROBLEM

LIFE PROHIBITED
UNDER PENALTY
OF LAW
L.B.M.C. 666-156

The SOLUTION

◆◆◆◆◆◆◆◆◆◆◆◆◆◆◆◆◆◆◆◆◆◆◆◆◆◆◆◆◆◆

HOW TO HAVE A HAPPY DAY

◆◆◆◆◆◆◆◆◆◆◆◆◆◆◆◆◆◆◆◆◆◆◆◆◆◆◆◆◆◆

HYATT'S TRIPOLAR FORMULA FOR SUCCESS

1. Have some Fun
2. Make some Money
3. Do some Good along the Way

(Not Necessarily in that Order!)

It is difficult to know how anything will turn out. Disappointments can dash your hopes, throw you in despair — Feeling Bad -- STILL SHINING

The new Human will be able to Live without having to have an explanation.

A sign of intelligence has always been an answer to a question. The truth or error of the answer is always a function of the good taste of the inquisitor.

The sign of true genius is understanding why there is a question in the first place.

Man appears to have a need for Final Goals, ends in themselves, the curse of Kant's (Thing in itself).

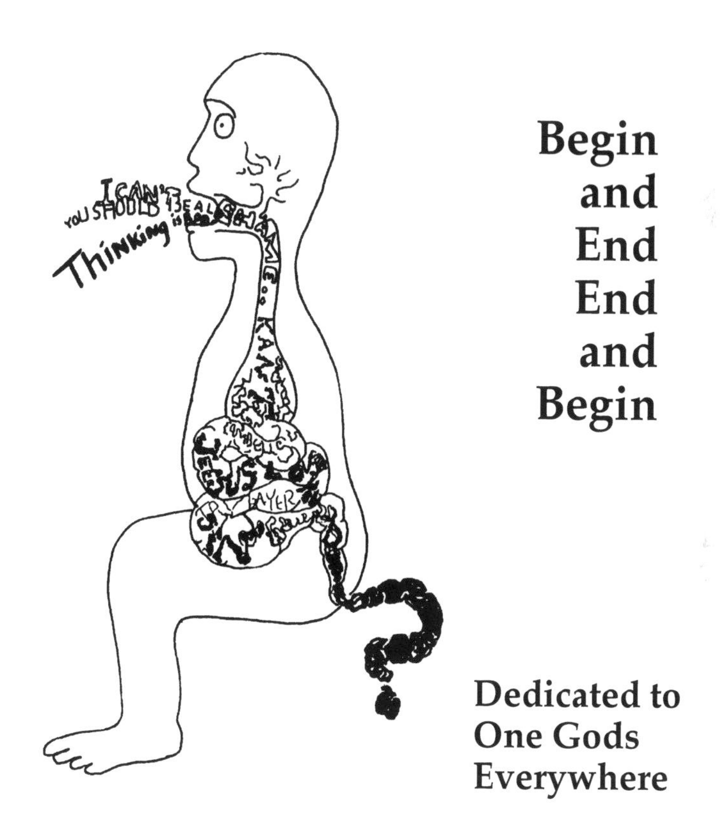

Begin
and
End
End
and
Begin

Dedicated to
One Gods
Everywhere

Could this be a Curse of the Digestive process?

The New Human will prefer to:

LIVE IN THE

TERROR

OF THE

RATHER

THAN

THE

BLISS

OF

THE

●

"In the END ...
a cymbal is just
a LOUD NOISE !"

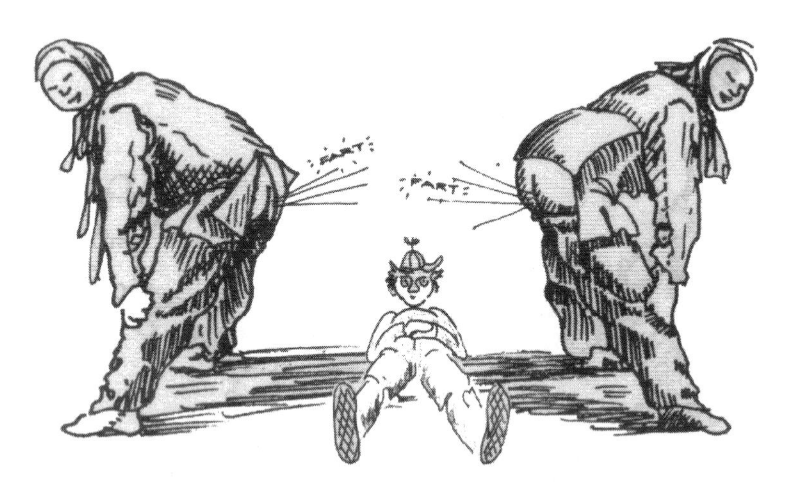

HYATT LOOKING
FOR METAPHYSICIANS

The human race has striven to set itself at odds with itself.

To put things a little straighter I have formulated the following definition. Please feel free to agree or disagree; however, it is important that an alternative be considered if you reject what follows:

HYATT'S NUMBER ONE PROPOSITION FOR FUTURE MUTANTS

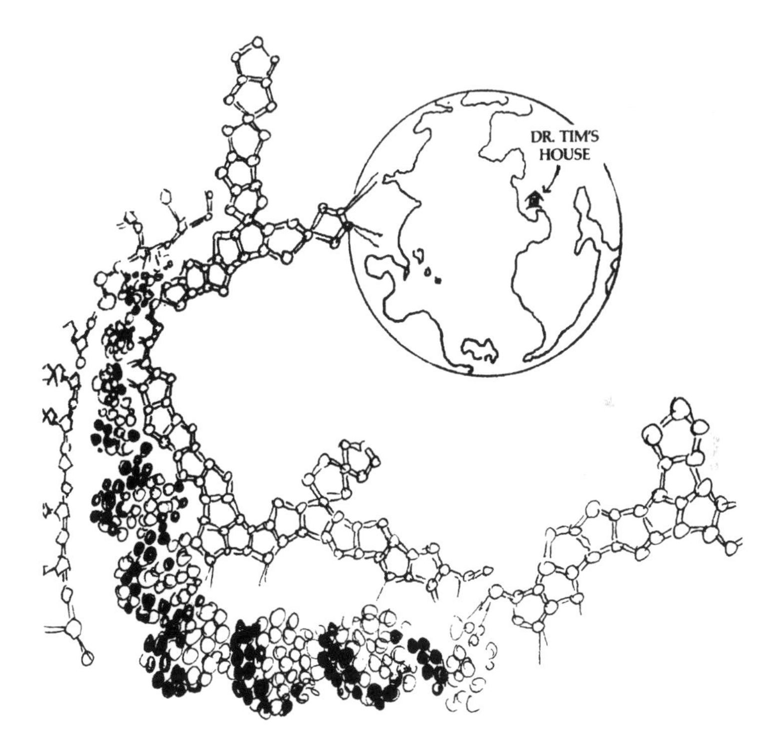

CULTURE IS THE RESULT OF THE INTERACTION
OF GENETICS AND GEOGRAPHY

Round houses, square houses, shoes, clothes, gathering, planting, religion, mating, child rearing, etc., all begin as a result of a set of genes in an environment. From this point evolves a set of trials/errors/successes which in turn begin to affect the environment and the genetic structure.

Although there are a variety of possible trials/errors/successes, the Initial ones become dogma for a genetic structure with language-cortex.

As all genes within a pool are not alike, and as the initial successes/errors change the context, different trials are attempted which either succeed or err at the time.

As genetics and geography are manipulated by the Farber-Silicon-Mush, earlier solutions (Dogma) and Priest-Reps experience fear and trembling and use the forces which they have accumulated to destroy, modify, repackage, include new trials/ successes/failures.

$$M = \frac{\Sigma_0^\infty}{0} = 0$$

This is known as statistics, the science of the STATE.

The difference between Dogma AND successes/ failures is that Dogma HAS BECOME normative and TSF are instrumental. Old successes/failures become dogma for present and future successes/ failures.

The Command is: SUCCEED AT ANY COST
The Injunction is: AT NO COST SUCCEED

The result is, of course, conflict, anxiety, a lack of moral sureness, loss of self-esteem, a disowning of self and the creation of:

AN IMAGE which is for show
and A BEAST whose hungers never end.

CHECK THE M̄, BUT FIRST
YOU MUST GET A LAW °

This split leads to alcoholism, drug addiction, divorce, rape, theft, murder, dis-ease, stress, neurosis, psychosis, etc. Neither the instrumental philosophy nor the Normative Philosophy can for long tolerate these "failures" as, after a period of time, they lead to revolution.

As an attempt to cope, they impose laws, treatment of the offender, etc., never for one moment considering the possibility that they are the culprits, the cause for the breakdown in the re-productive-birth-death-hereafter assembly line.

Like the Mercedes Benz symbol, ideologies summarize a morass of feelings and associations. However, the symbol for a Mercedes Benz is not the car. It is no longer even a sign for recognizing the manufacturer. Now what is important are the associations of status, good taste, wealth, intelligence, etc. which the symbol has been made to represent. This is rhetoric and hallucinatory. I call this intimidation by SYMBOL.

THE LONGS AND THE SHORTS OF IT.

POOR SCHNOOK BELIEVED IN WALL STREET!

For example, Yuppies are now the symbol of sophistication as Money—according to one noted observer—is the primary goal. Money IS sophistication.

To quote Crowley:

"MONEY MONEY MONEY MONEY MONEY MONEY MONEY MONEY MONEY MONEY MONEY MONEY MONEY MONEY MONEY"

M.B.A. is a cymbal for expert. Note, M.B.A.'s do come from Harvard as well as Y U BUM State. Is a Harvard M.B.A., in fact, better? If we employ status, the answer is YES. HARVARD is KNOWN, has been AROUND for a Long Time, which is, of course, "real" proof of its Value. So what if Y U BUM State is teaching "inverse-multi-variate-laser-digital analysis of win/lose strategies" which predicts outcomes 93% of the time, while Harvard's methods only work 66.6% of the time?

Yuppies have taken the once hated materialism and turned it into a SPIRITUAL GOLD. They have created an ideology and are busy worshipping at the altar. DO NOT DISTURB!

Now, Dr. Hyatt, who is kidding whom?

A TRANCE IS NO DEEPER THAN YOU ARE

It is amazing how sure a stupid person can be. It is amazing how sure an Interior Decorator can be. It is amazing how sure a FURNITURE BUYER IS!

A TRANCE IS NO DEEPER THAN YOU ARE

Take none of this very seriously. Who can compete with a man/woman who knows how to dress themselves and use vel-crow. Who can compete with someone who spends two hours a day doing His hair?

If you're IN you're IN, and if you're OUT you're IN.

IS THIS THE BEGINNING
OR IS IT THE END?

The Clock is Ticking

LEARY UNIVERSITY
OR
I A TOL A U

FREEDOM HARD PEACE ANGER JOY SEX SEX SEX SEX SEX REALITY SECURITY GOD EVIL DEATH PAIN

DO YOU WANT TO BE INVISIBLE?

ROLES MODELS WORDS WORDS WORDS CONFUSION CLARITY FUNCTION WORK CAREER GOOD SPORT SENSE OF HUMOR JOKES UNDERSTANDING HALLUCINATIONS QUESTIONS FUN SEX BODY MOTHER COUNTRY UFO STRONG POWER SOFT POSITIVE FREEDOM HARD PEACE ANGER JOY SEX SEX SEX SEX SEX REALITY SECURITY GOD EVIL DEATH PAIN PLEASURE NEGATIVE SEX DISEASE HEALTH PROSPERITY SEDUCTION MONEY PET STEREOTYPES ROLES MODELS WORDS WORDS WORDS CONFUSION CLARITY FUNCTION WORK CAREER GOOD SPORT SENSE OF HUMOR JOKES UNDERSTANDING HALLUCINATIONS QUESTIONS ALIEN FUN SEX SOFT POWER HARD LOYALTY PEACE WISDOM SECRETS MYTH BLOOD PURITY ORGASM FREEDOM MANIPULATION CONTROL MEN SONS FREEDOM FATHER SOFT HARD LOYALTY COMFORT SECURITY REALITY FANTASY PLEASURE HOME CAREER BE ALL THAT YOU CAN BE SUPER WOMAN WONDER WOMAN POWERFUL WOMAN BE ALL THAT YOU CAN BE BE ALL THAT YOU CAN BE BE ALL THAT YOU CAN BE ALL ALL ALL YOU YOU YOU YOU CAN YOU CAN YOU CAN YOU CAN LEADER FOLLOWER YOU ARE ALL THAT YOU CAN BE YOU ARE WHAT YOU ARE WHAT? YOU ARE ARE ARE ARE ARE ARE ARE

LOYALTY FEMININE LOVE BAD WEALTH JUSTICE FUN SEX BODY MOTHER COUNTRY UFO STRONG POWER SOFT POSITIVE FREEDOM HARD PEACE

LEARN HOW TO LEARN HOW TO

WISH DESIRE SATISFACTION CHILDREN FREEDOM ALIEN FUN SEX SOFT POWER HARD LOYALTY PEACE WISDOM SECRETS MYTH BLOOD PURITY ORGASM FREEDOM MANIPULATION CONTROL MEN SONS FREEDOM FATHER SOFT HARD LOYALTY COMFORT SECURITY REALITY FANTASY PLEASURE HOME CAREER BE ALL THAT YOU CAN BE SUPER WOMAN WONDER WOMAN POWERFUL WOMAN GODDESS SON OF GOD GURU SHRINK LUNACY REST FREEDOM SUPPORT LACK FULLNESS WORK PLEASURE GAIN PAIN SOLIDARITY ETHNIC SECRETS BLOOD BODY POWER FEMININE CUT BEAUTY LOVE HATE LUST GREED BAD GIRL WANT DESIRES POWER FREEDOM GOD EVIL DEATH PAIN GOOD WEAK SEX MASCU-LINE PAIN DRUGS LOVE BAD WEALTH NEGATIVE RADIANT LOYALTY UFO FEMININE JUSTICE FUN SEX BODY MOTHER PEACE FREEDOM SOFT POSITIVE FREEDOM HARD ANGER ANSWER JOY HAPPINESS SEX SECURITY CAREER WORK FAMILY HOME FOOD FAT IMAGE BODY PERFECT IDEAL STRAIGHT TWISTED CRAZY HELP SECURITY NEUROTIC HEALTHY SANITY DISEASED LOYALTY FEMININE LOVE BAD WEALTH JUSTICE FUN SEX BODY MOTHER COUNTRY UFO STRONG POWER SOFT POSITIVE

WALK THROUGH WORDS

HIRE and FIRE your IDOLS

For your official GOD FORMS, see

A Modern Shaman's Guide to a Pregnant Universe
by Christopher S. Hyatt and Antero Alli

THE IMMORTALITY OPTION

by Camden Benares

When I wrote *Zen Without Zen Masters*, I included the following information: "The only dimension of life over which you have limited control is the length. By putting your attention on what you do to extend your life, you can utilize the potential you have for its duration. But be aware that every day you control the depth and width of your experience, your life." Now there is an immortalist movement to extend life's duration to infinity—to put immortality within the human grasp.

What do these immortalists have in common? They are optimistic about the human condition. They are interested in the future where all of us will live our lives of whatever length. They believe that immortality is a goal worthy of the greatest possible effort.

Although I am not an immortalist, I see the value in immortality research. To extend life means strengthening the human immune system and ending the threat of diseases that end life or erode the quality of life.

Years ago I read a short story about beings from outer space arriving on Earth. When asked their intentions, they replied that they had come to conquer the enemy. The human assured the aliens that Earth was peaceful and had no enemy. The aliens said that the enemy was what the humans called death. That was my first exposure to the immortalist viewpoint and I felt the power of the idea of living forever.

Since then, as an occasional reader and writer of science fiction, I've read about immortality and considered writing about how immortals would live in a possible near future.

Each writer has a different answer to some of the more perplexing aspects of immortality, such as: How will the immortals deal with the mortals who oppose them on political, philosophical or other grounds? If immortality is not available for everyone, what selection process will be used? How will immortality affect the mores, folkways, ideas and daily life of society?

Until space migration is a realistic solution to the population explosion, many people will see immortals as a new addition to the conditions that threaten the quality of human life. That is why the optimism of the immortalists is desperately needed to inspire and sponsor research into new approaches to solving the problems that the pessimists and realists have defined. To change the world from a place where millions of unwanted children grow up to be unwanted adults requires the kind of determination that can stem from intelligent, applied optimism. The kind of world in which immortality can be a viable reality is the kind of a world where human life is worth more than the price of a cartridge or the cost of a bomb. The courage to work toward such a world where there is reverence for life is a hallmark of the immortalist.

Those who hold views about death that differ from those of the immortalists must be informed that immortalists are not their enemies. The work that the immortalists want to do holds genuine hope for making this world a better place in which to live. It is in the long-range, intelligent, self-interest of humans to do that. The immortalists are volunteers, willing to work to improve the human condition. I believe that anyone interested in helping humanity has chosen a valid path. I applaud those who seek the immortality option.

WHY DOES DR. HYATT WORSHIP AT THE IDOL OF ERROR

As we find ultimate Error
our abhorrence for Truth
will become
Self Evident

FLASH! FLASH! FLASH! FLASH!
NEWS RELEASE

!!!!!! IMMORTALITY IS 666 DAYS AWAY !!!!!!
3.2 Billion People Commit Suicide
To Save Face for Being in Error

"Scientists discover Planet Zingo beyond Pluto. Intelligent communication received. 'It was all a hoax, there is NO Life After Death.' That notion was orchestrated by 'Jesus Christ Smith,' a lower echelon pilot on suspension for drug abuse."

("That line is OK, but kinda corny," sez Dr. Tim.)

As a result of this, a special session of the UN was convened and it was unanimously decided to divert all educational, defense, highway, moral and social security funds to immortality research.

All religious leaders of the world are forced to seek employment. The Pope is kicked out of the Vatican, and the structure is refurbished into a LAB. He is now a Bag Lady in Santa Monica.

REDECORATING
IS
HARD
WORK
!!!

TWENTY-TWO ALTERNATIVES TO INVOLUNTARY DEATH

by Timothy Leary, Ph.D. & Eric Gullichsen

"Death is the ultimate negative patient health outcome."

— William L. Roper, Director,
Health Care Financing Administration (HCFA),
which administers Medicare

Most human beings face death with an "attitude" of helplessness, either resigned or fearful. Neither of these submissive, often uninformed, "angles of approach" to the most crucial event of one's life can be ennobling.

Today, there are many practical options available for dealing with the dying process. Passivity, failure to learn about them, might be the ultimate irretrievable blunder. Pascal's famous no-lose wager about the existence of God translates into modern life as a no-risk gamble on the prowess of technology.

For millennia the fear of death has depreciated individual confidence and increased dependence on authority.

True, the loyal member of a familial or racial gene-pool can take pride in the successes and survival tenacity of their kin-ship.

But for the individual, the traditional prospects are less than exalted. Let's be laser-honest here. How can you be proud of your past achievements, walk tall in the present or zap enthusiastically into the future if, awaiting you implacably around some future corner, is Old Mr. D., The Grim Reaper?

What a PR job the Word Makers did to build this Death Concept into a Prime-Time Horror Show! The grave. Mortification. Extinction. Breakdown. Catastrophe. Doom. Finish. Fatality. Malignancy. Necrology. Obituary. The End.

Note the calculated negativity. To die is to croak, to give up the ghost, to bite the dust, to kick the bucket, to perish. To become inanimate, lifeless, defunct, extinct, moribund, cadaverous, necrotic. A corpse, a stiff, a cadaver, a relic, food for worms, a corpus delicti, a carcass. What a miserable ending to the game of life!

Fear of Death Was an Evolutionary Necessity in the Past

In the past, the reflexive genetic duty of TOP MANAGEMENT (those in social control of the various gene-pools) has been to make humans feel weak, helpless, and dependent in the face of death. The good of the race or nation was ensured at the cost of the sacrifice of the individual.

Obedience and submission was rewarded on a time-payment plan. For his/her devotion the individual was promised immortality in the postmortem hive-center variously known as "heaven," "paradise," or the "Kingdom of the Lord." In order to maintain the attitude of dedication, the gene-pool managers had to control the "dying reflexes," orchestrate the trigger-stimuli that activate the "death circuits" of the brain. This was accomplished through rituals that imprint dependence and docility when the "dying alarm bells" go off in the brain.

Perhaps we can better understand this imprinting mechanism by considering another set of "rituals," those by which human hives manage the conception-reproduction reflexes. A discussion of these is less likely to alarm you. And the mechanisms of control imposed by the operation of social machinery are similar in the two cases. We invite you to "step outside the system" for a moment, to vividly see what is ordinarily invisible because it is so entrenched in our expectation.

At adolescence each kinship group provides rituals, taboos, ethical prescriptions to guide the all-important sperm-egg situation.

Management by the individual of the horny DNA machinery is always a threat to hive inbreeding. Dress, grooming, dating, courtship, contraception, and abortion patterns are fanatically conventionalized in tribal and feudal societies. Personal innovation is sternly condemned and ostracized. Industrial democracies vary in the sexual freedom allowed individuals. But in totalitarian states, China and Iran for example, rigid prudish morality controls the mating reflexes and governs boy-girl relations. Under the Chinese dictator Mao, "romance" was forbidden because it weakened dedication to the state, i.e., the local gene-pool. If teen-agers pilot and select their own mating, then they will be more likely to fertilize outside the hive, more likely to insist on directing their own lives, and, worst of all, less likely to rear their offspring with blind gene-pool loyalty.

Even more rigid social-imprinting rituals guard the "dying reflexes." Hive control of "death" responses is taken for granted in all pre-cybernetic societies.

In the past this conservative degradation of individuality was an evolutionary virtue.

During epochs of species stability, when the tribal, feudal and industrial technologies were being mastered and fine-tuned, wisdom was centered in the gene-pool stored in the collective linguistic-consciousness, the racial data-base of the hive.

Since individual life was short, brutish, aimless, what a singular learned was nearly irrelevant. The world was changing so slowly that knowledge could only be embodied in the species. Lacking the technologies for the personal mastery of transmission and storage of information, the individual was simply too slow, too small, to matter. Loyalty to the racial collective was the virtue. Creativity, Premature Individuation, was anti-evolutionary. A weirdo, mutant distraction. Only Village Idiots would try to commit independent, unauthorized thought.

In the feudal and industrial eras, Management used the fear of death to motivate and control individuals. Today, politicians use the death-dealing military and the police and capital punishment to protect the social order. Organized religion maintains its power and wealth by orchestrating and exaggerating the fear of death.

Among the many things that the Pope, the Ayatollah, and Fundamentalist Protestants agree on: confident understanding and self-directed mastery of the dying process is the last thing to be allowed to the individual. The very notion of Cybernetic Post-Biological Intelligence or consumer immortality-options is taboo, sinful. For formerly valid reasons of gene-pool protection.

Religions have cleverly monopolized the rituals of dying to increase control over the superstitious. Throughout history the priests and mullahs have swarmed around the expiring human like black vultures. Death belonged to them.

As we grow up in the 20th century we are systematically programmed about How to Die. Hospitals are staffed with priests/ministers/rabbis ready to perform the "last rites." Every army unit has its Catholic Chaplain to administer the Sacrament of Extreme Unction (what a phrase, really!) to the expiring soldier. The Ayatollah, Chief Mullah of the Islamic Death Cult, sends his teenage soldiers into the Iraq minefields with dog-tags guaranteeing immediate transfer to the Allah's Destination Resort. Koranic Heaven. A terrible auto crash? Call the medics! Call the priest! Call the Reverend!

In the Industrial Society, everything becomes part of Big Business. Dying involves Blue Cross, Medicare, Health Care Delivery Systems, the Health Care Financing Administration (HCFA), terminal patient wards. Undertakers. Cemeteries. The funeral rituals.

The monopolies of religion and the assembly lines of Top Management process the dying and the dead even more efficiently than the living.

We recall that knowledge and selective choice about such gene-pool issues as conception, test-tube fertilization, pregnancy, abortion is dangerous enough to the church-fathers.

But suicide, right-to-die concepts, euthanasia, life-extension, out-of-the-body experiences, occult experimentation, astral-travel scenarios, death/rebirth reports, extra-terrestrial speculation, cryogenics, sperm-banks, egg-banks, DNA banks, personally-empowering Artificial Intelligence Technology—anything that encourages the individual to engage in personal speculation and experimentation with immortality—is anathema to the orthodox Seed-Shepherds of the feudal and industrial ages.

Why? Because if the flock doesn't fear death, then the grip of Religious and Political Management is broken. The power of the gene-pool is threatened. And when control loosens in the gene-pool, dangerous genetic innovations and mutational visions tend to emerge.

Some believe that the Cybernetic Age we are entering could mark the beginning of a period of enlightened and intelligent individualism, a time unique in history when technology is available to individuals to support a huge diversity of personalized lifestyles and cultures, a world of diverse, interacting social groups whose initial-founding membership number is one.[1]

The exploding technology of computation and communication lays a delicious feast of knowledge and personal choice within our easy grasp. Under such conditions, the operating wisdom and control naturally passes from aeons-old power of gene pools, and locates in the rapidly self-modifying brains of individuals capable of dealing with an ever-accelerating rate of change.

Aided by customized, personally-programmed quantum-linguistic appliances, the individual can choose his/her own social and genetic future. And perhaps choose not to "die".

---

[1] The authors divide the stages of human history into: tribal, feudal, industrial, and cybernetic.

The Wave Theory of Evolution

Current theories of genetics suggest that evolution, like everything else in the universe, comes in waves.

So, at times of Punctuated Evolution, collective metamorphosis, when many things are mutating at the same time, then the ten commandments of the "old ones" become ten more suggestions...

At such times of rapid innovation and collective mutation, conservative hive dogma can be dangerous, suicidal. Individual experimentation and exploration, the thoughtful methodical scientific challenging of taboos, becomes the key to the survival of the gene-school.

Now, as we enter the Cybernetic Age, we arrive at a new wisdom which broadens our definition of personal immortality and gene-pool survival: *The Post-Biological Options of the Information Species.* A fascinating set of gourmet-consumer choices suddenly appear on the pop-up menu of The Evolutionary Cafe.

It is beginning to look as though in the Information Society, the individual human being can script, produce, direct his/her own immortality.

Here we face Mutation Shock in its most panicky form. And, as we have done in understanding earlier mutations, the first step is to develop a new language. We should not impose the values or vocabulary of the past species upon the new Cybernetic Culture.

Would you let the buzz-words of a preliterate paleolithic cult control your life? Will you let the superstitions of a tribal-village culture (now represented by the Pope and the Ayatollah) shuffle you off the scene? Will you let the mechanical planned-obsolescence tactics of the Factory Culture manage your existence?

So let us have no more pious wimp-sheep talk about death. The time has come to talk cheerfully and joke sassily about personal responsibility for managing the dying process. For starters let's de-mystify death and develop alternative metaphors for consciousness leaving the body. Let us speculate good-naturedly about post-biological options. Let's be bold about opening up a broad spectrum of Club-Med post-biological possibilities.

For starters, let's replace the word "death" with the more neutral, precise, scientific term: *Metabolic Coma.* And then let's go on to suggest that this temporary state of "coma" might be replaced by: *Auto-Metamorphosis,* a self-controlled change in bodily form, where the individual chooses to change his/her vehicle of existence without loss of consciousness.

Then, let's distinguish between involuntary and voluntary metabolic coma. Reversible and irreversible dying.

Let's explore that fascinating "no man's land"—the period between body-death and neurological-death in terms of the knowledge-information processing involved.

And let's collect some data about that even more intriguing zone now beginning to be researched in the cross-disciplinary field of scientific study known as Artificial Life.[2] What knowledge-information processing capacities can be preserved after both metabolic coma and brain cessation? What natural and artificial systems, from the growth of mineral structures to the self-reproduction of formal mathematical automata, are promising alternative candidates to biology for the support of life?

And then let us perform the ultimate act of Human Intelligence. Let's venture with calm, open-minded tolerance and scientific rigor into that perennially mysterious *terra incognita* and ask the final question: What knowledge-information processing possibilities can remain after the

---

2 Los Alamos, famous as the birthplace of atomic weapons, today also houses the Center for Nonlinear Studies, where a group has been meeting weekly to discuss the many technical aspects of the newly identified field of Artificial Life. The center recently sponsored a week-long international workshop, the world's first, where scientists met to discuss the implications and craft the foundational theories of the field.

The meeting was friendly, fun, and wildly trans-disciplinary. Nanotechnology pioneers outlined the potential for protein engineering, and robotics expert Hans Moravec presented compelling arguments that a genetic takeover was underway, our cultural artifacts now evolving past the point of symbiosis with the human species. Self-replicating structures ranging from minerals to computer viruses were demonstrated.

cessation of all biological life: somatic, neurological and genetic?

How can human consciousness be supported in hardware outside the moist envelope of graceful, attractive, pleasure-filled meat we now inhabit? How can the organic, carbon-constructed caterpillar become the silicon butterfly?

C.S. Hyatt, Ph.D. and A.K. O'Shea have suggested three stages of *Post-Biological Intelligence:*

1. *Cybernetic Recognition* of the myriad knowledge-information processing varieties involved in the many stages of dying.
2. *Cybernetic Management:* Developing knowledge-information processing skills while out-of-body, out-of-brain and beyond DNA.
3. *Cybernetic-Technological,* Attaining one, or many, of the immortality options.

Post-Biological Recognition Intelligence

We recognize that the dying process, for millennia has been blanketed by taboo and primitive superstition, has suddenly become accessible to human intelligence.

Here we experience the sudden insights that we need not "go quietly" and passively into the dark night or the neon-lit, musak-enhanced Disney-heaven of the PTL crowd. We realize that the concept of involuntary, irreversible metabolic coma known as death is a feudal superstition, a marketing efficiency of industrial society. We understand that one can discover dozens of active, creative alternatives to going belly-up clutching the company logo of the Christian Cross, Blue Cross, Crescent Cross, or the eligibility cards of the Veterans Administration.

Recognition is always the beginning of the possibility for change. Once we comprehend that "death" can be defined as a problem of knowledge-information processing, solutions to this age-long "problem" can emerge. One realizes that the intelligent thing to do is to try to keep one's knowledge-processing capacities around as long as possible. In bodily form. In neural form. In the silicon circuitry and magnetic storage media of today's computers. In molecular form, through the atom-stacking of nanotechnology in tomorrow's computers. In cryogenic form. In the form of stored data, legend, myth. In the form of off-spring who are cybernetically trained to use Post Biological Intelligence. In the form of post-biological gene-pools, info-pools, advanced viral forms resident in world computer networks and cyberspace matrices of the sort described in the "sprawl novels" of William Gibson.[3]

The second step in attaining *Post-Biological Recognition Intelligence* is to shift from the passive to the active mode. Industrial age humans were trained to await docilely the onset of termination and then to turn over their body for disposal to the priests and the factory (hospital) technicians.

Our species is now developing the Cybernetic Information Skills to plan ahead, to make one's will prevail. The smart thing to do is to see dying as a change in the implementation of information-processing: to orchestrate it, manage it, anticipate and exercise the many available options.

We consider here twenty-two distinct methods of avoiding a submissive or fearful dying.[4]

Post-Biological Programming Intelligence

Elsewhere the authors have defined 8 levels of intelligence: biological emotional, mental-symbolic, social, aesthetic, neurological-cybernetic, genetic, atomic-nano-tech. At each stage there is a recognition stage, followed by a brain-programming or brain-reprogramming stage.

In order to re-program it is necessary to activate the circuits in the brain which mediate that particular dimension of intelligence. Once this circuit is "turned on" it is possible to re-imprint or re-program.

---

[3] William Gibson, cyberpunk psy-fi visionary, has published *Neuromancer, Count Zero* and *Burning Chrome.* They are recommended reading for their technically and socially plausible vision of high-tech low-life on the streets.

[4] Mystics may remark that there are also 22 paths in the Kabbalistic "Tree of Life" associated with the Tarot.

Cognitive neurology suggests that the most direct way to re-program emotional responses is to re-activate the appropriate circuits. To reprogram sexual responses it is effective to re-activate and re-experience the original teenage imprints and re-imprint new sexual responses.

The circuits of the brain which mediate the "dying" process are routinely experienced during "near-death" crises. For centuries people have reported: "My entire life flashed before my eyes as I sank for the third time."

This "near-death" experience can be "turned-on" via the relevant anesthetic drugs. Ketamine, for example.

Or by learning enough about the effects of out-of-the-body drugs so that one can use hypnotic techniques to activate the desired circuits without using external chemical stimuli.

We see immediately that the rituals intuitively developed by religious groups are designed to induce trance states related to "dying." The child growing up in a Catholic culture is deeply imprinted (programmed) by funeral rites. The arrival of the solemn priest to administer extreme unction becomes an access code for the *Post-Biological* state. Other cultures have different rituals for activating and then controlling (programming) the death circuits of the brain. Until recently, very few have permitted personal control or customized consumer choice.

Perhaps this discussion of the "dying circuits of the brain" is too innovative. Sometimes it is easier to understand new concepts about one's own species by referring to other species. Almost every animal species manifests "dying reflexes." Some animals leave the herd to die alone. Others stand with legs apart, stolidly postponing the last moment. Some species eject the dying organism from the social group.

To gain navigational control of one's dying processes three steps suggest themselves: 1) activate the death-reflexes imprinted by your culture, experience them… 2) trace their origins, and… 3) re-program.

The aim is to develop a scientific model of the chain of cybernetic (knowledge-information) processes that occur as one approaches this metamorphic stage—and to intentionally develop options for taking active responsibility for these events.

Achieving Immortality

Since the dawn of human history, philosophers and theologians have speculated about immortality. Uneasy, aging kings have commanded methods for extending the life span.

A most dramatic example of this age-long impulse is ancient Egypt which produced mummification, the pyramids and manuals like the *Egyptian Book of the Dying.*

The Tibetan Book of the Dying (Buddhist) presents a masterful model of post-mortem stages and techniques for guiding the student to a state of immortality which is neurologically "real" and suggests scientific techniques for reversing the dying process.

The new field of molecular engineering is producing techniques within the framework of current consensus Western Science to implement auto-metamorphosis.

The aim of the game is to defeat death—to give the Individual mastery of this, the final stupidity.

The next section of this essay presents twenty-two methods of achieving immortality. We do not especially endorse any particular technique. Our aim is to review all options and encourage creative-courageous thinking about new possibilities.

A PRELIMINARY LIST OF IMMORTALITY OPTIONS (To Replace Involuntary-Irreversible Metabolic Coma)

I. Psychological/Behavioral Training Techniques

The techniques in this category do not assist in attaining personal immortality per se, but are useful in acquiring the experience of "experimental dying," reversible-voluntary exploration of the territory between body-coma and brain, death, sometimes called out-of-body experiences; or near-dying experiences. Others have termed these astral travel, or reincarnation memories.

1. Meditation & Hypnosis.

These are the classic yogic routes to exploration of non-ordinary states of consciousness. They are well known to be labor and time intensive. For the most intelligent and comprehensive discussion of these techniques, we recommend Crowley.[5]

2. Carefully Designed Psychedelic Drug Experiences of "Dying" & Genetic (Re-Incarnation/Pre-Incarnation) Consciousness.

There is, here, no commitment to any occultist theory about biological incarnation. We refer to techniques enabling access to information and operational programs stored in the brain of the individual. In normal states of consciousness, these are subroutines operating below voluntary access.[6]

3. Experimental Out-Of-Body Experiences Using Anesthetics.

John Lilly has written extensively about his experiences with small dosages of anesthetics such as Ketamine.[7] It is possible that the out-of-body subjective effects of such substances are (merely) interpretations of proprioceptive disruption. Nevertheless, Lilly's reported experiences seem to indicate that information is available through these investigative routes.

4. Sensory Deprivation/Isolation Tanks.

Again, Lilly has investigated this subject most comprehensively.[8]

---

[5] Aleister Crowley, *Eight Lectures on Yoga.* (Divided into two parts respectively entitled, "Yoga for Yahoos," and "Yoga for Yellowbellies.")

[6] Marvin Minsky has outlined a theory that "mind" emerges from a collection of smaller interacting entities, themselves mindless. This is outlined in his book *The Society of Mind,* Simon & Schuster, 1986.

[7] John Lilly, *The Scientist,* and *Programming & Metaprogramming in the Human Biocomputer.*

[8] John Lilly, *The Deep Self.*

5. Re-Programming Exercises (Suspending the Effects of & Replacing Early "Death" Imprints Imposed By Culture).

6. Development of New Rituals to Guide the Post-Body Transition.

Our cultural taboos have prohibited the development of much detailed work in this area. One of the few available sources in this area is E.J. Gold.[9]

7. Pre-Incarnation Exercises.

With these, one uses the preferred altered state method (drugs, hypnosis, shamanic trance, voodoo ritual, born-again frenzies) to create future scripts for oneself.

8. Aesthetically-Orchestrated Voluntary "Dying".

This procedure has been called suicide, i.e., "self-murder," by officials who wish to control the mortem process. Mr. and Mrs. Arthur Koestler, active members of the British EXIT program arranged a most dignified and graceful voluntary metabolic coma. A California group, HADDA, is placing an amendment on California ballot to permit terminal patients to plan voluntary metacom with their medical advisors.

The non-Californian can always look for an enlightened MD, or consenting adult friends to act as guides to the Western Lands.

II. Somatic Techniques for Life Extension

Techniques to inhibit the process of aging comprise the classical approach to immortality. In the present state of science, these "buy time."

9. Diet.

The classic research on diet-and-longevity has been performed by Roy L. Walford, M.D.[10]

---

[9] E.J. Gold *American Book of the Dead.* IDHHB, 1973. See also Gold's *Creation Story.*

[10] Roy L. Walford, M.D. *The 120 Year Diet,* Simon & Schuster, 1986 and *Maximum Life Span,* W.W. Norton, New York 1983.

10. Life-Extension Drugs.

These include anti-oxidants et al. A comprehensive reference is *Life Extension* by Sandy Shaw and Durk Pearson.

11. Exercise Regimes.

12. Temperature Variation.

13. Sleep Treatments (Hibernation).

14. Immunization to Counter the Aging Process.

III. Somatic/Neural/Genetic Preservation

Techniques in this class do not ensure continuous operation of consciousness. They produce potentially reversible metabolic coma. They are alternatives for preserving the structure of tissues until a time of more advanced medical knowledge.

15. Cryogenics or Vacuum-Pack "Pickling."

Why let one's body and brain rot, when that seems to imply no possibility at all for your future? Why let the carefully arranged tangle of dendritic growths in your nervous system which may be the storage site for all of your memories get eaten by fungus? Perpetual preservation of your tissues is available today at moderate cost.[11]

16. Cryonic Preservation of Neural Tissue or DNA.

Those not particularly attached to their bodies can opt for preservation of the essentials: their brains together with the instructional codes capable of regrowing something genetically identical to their present bio-machinery.

IV. Bio-Genetic Methods for Life Extension

Is there any need to experience metabolic coma at all? We have mentioned ways to gain personal control of the experience, to stave it off by "conventional" longevity techniques, to avoid irreversible dissolution of the systemic substrate.

---

[11] One of the few cryogenic preservation companies in operation is the Alcor Foundation, (800) 367-2228.

Techniques are now emerging to permit a much more vivid guarantee of personal persistence, a smooth metamorphic transformation into a different form of substrate on which the computer program of consciousness runs.

17. Cellular/DNA Repair.

Nanotechnology is the science and engineering of mechanical and electronic systems built at atomic dimensions.[12] One forecast ability of nanotechnology is its potential for production of self-replicating nano-machines living within individual biological cells.

These artificial enzymes will effect cellular repair, as damage occurs from mechanical causes, radiation, or other aging effects. Repair of DNA ensures genetic stability.

18. Cloning.

Biologically-based replication of genetically identical personal copies of yourself, at any time desired, is approaching the possible. Sex is fun, but sexual reproduction is biologically inefficient, suited mainly for inducing genetic variation in species which still advance through the accidents of luck in random combination.

---

[12] The most visible and eloquent proponent of nanotechnology is K. Eric Drexler of MIT and Stanford Universities. His book *Engines of Creation* provides a detailed overview of the field. Other more technical works include:

K. Eric Drexler, *Molecular Engineering: An Approach to the Development of General Capabilities for Molecular Manipulation,* Proc. Natl. Acad. Sci USA, Vol. 78 #9, September 1981 pp. 5275–5278.

K. Eric Drexler, *Rod Logic & Thermal Noise in the Mechanical Nanocomputer,* Proc. 3rd Intl. Symposium on Molecular Electronic Devices, Elsevier North Holland, 1987.

K. Eric Drexler, *Molecular Engineering: Assemblers and Future Space Hardware,* Aerospace XXI, 33rd Annual meeting of the American Astronautical Society, paper AAS-86–415.

Feynman, R. "There's Plenty of Room at the Bottom," in *Miniaturization,* H.D. Gilbert (ed.), Reinhold, New York, 1961 pp. 282–296. One of the original works approaching molecular-scale engineering. Nobel prize winner Feynman is without a doubt one of the most brilliant scientists of the century.

V. Cybernetic (Post-Biological) Methods for Attaining Immortality [Artificial Life in Silicon]

As the neuromantic cyberpunk author Bruce Sterling notes, evolution moves in clades, radiating outward in omni-directional diversity, and not following a single linear path. Some silicon visionaries believe that natural evolution of the human species (or at least their branch of it) is near completion. They are no longer interested in merely procreating, but in designing their successors. Carnegie-Mellon robot scientist Hans Moravec writes:

> *We owe our existence to organic evolution. But we owe it little loyalty. We are on the threshold of a change in the universe comparable to the transition from non-life, to life.*[13]

Human society has now reached a turning point in the operation of the process of evolution, a point at which the next evolutionary step of the species is under our control. Or, more correctly, the next steps, which will occur in parallel, will result in an explosion of diversity of the human species. We are no longer dependent on fitness in any physical sense for survival, our quantum appliances and older mechanical devices provide the requisite means in all circumstances. In the near future, the (now merging) methods of computer and biological technology will make the human form a matter totally determined by individual choice.

As a flesh-and-blood species we are moribund, stuck at "a local optimum," to borrow a term from mathematical optimization theory.

Beyond this horizon, which humankind has reached, lies the unknown, the as-yet scarcely imagined. We will design our children, and co-evolve intentionally with the cultural artifacts which are our progeny.

Humans already come in some variety of races and sizes. In comparison to what "human" will mean within the next century, we humans are at present as indistinguishable from one another as are hydrogen molecules. Our anthropocentrism will decrease.

---

[13] Hans Moravec, *Mind Children,* 1988.

We see two principle categorizations of the form of the human of the future, one more biological-like: a bio-machine hybrid of any desired form, and one not biological at all: an "electronic life" on the computer networks. Human-as-machine, and human-in-machine.

Of these, human-as-machine is perhaps more easily conceived. Today we have crude prosthetic implants, artificial limbs, valves, and entire organs. Continuing improvements in old-style mechanical technology slowly increase the thoroughness of human-machine integration.

The electronic life form of human-in-machine is even more alien to our current conceptions of humanity. Through storage of one's belief systems as on-line data structures, driven by selected control structures (the electronic analog to will?), one's neuronal apparatus will operate in silicon as it did on the wetware of the brain, although faster, more accurately, more self-mutably, and, if desired, immortally.

19. Archival-Informational.

One standard way of becoming "immortal" is by leaving a trail of archives, biographies, and publicized noble deeds.

The increasing presence of stable knowledge media in our Cybernetic Society make this a more rigorous platform for persistent existence. The knowledge possessed by an individual is captured in expert systems, and world-scale hypertext systems[14] thus ensuring the longevity and accessibility of textural and graphical memes.

Viewed from outside the self, death is not a binary phenomenon, but a continuously varying function. How alive are you in Paris at this moment? In the city in which you live? In the room in which you are reading this?

---

[14] A world-scale hypertext system to permit instantaneous on-line access to global knowledge networks has been envisioned and written about by Ted Nelson, in *Literary Machines*, published by the author. Other information is available in Nelson's *Computer Lib* (1974), republished by Microsoft Press (1987).

20. *Head Coach* Personality Data Base Transmission.

Head Coach is a computer system under development by Futique Inc., one of the first examples of a new generation of psychoactive computer software. The program allows the user (performer) to digitize and store thoughts on a routine daily basis. If one leaves, let us say, 20 years of daily computer-stored records of thought-performance, one's grandchildren, a century down the line can "know" and replay your information habits and mental performances. They will be able to "share and relive experiences" in considerable detail. To take a most vulgar example, if an individual's moves in a chess game are stored, the descendants can relive, move-by-move, a game played by Great-Great-Grandmother in the past century.

As passive reading is replaced by "active re-writing," later generations will be able to relive how we performed the great books of our time.

Yet more intriguing is the possibility of implementing the knowledge extracted over time from a person: their beliefs, preferences, and tendencies, as a set of algorithms guiding a program capable of acting in a manner functionally identical to the person. Advances in robotics technology will take these "Turing creatures" away from being mere "brains in bottles" to hybrids capable of interacting sensorially with the physical world.

21. Nanotech Information Storage: Towards Direct Brain-Computer Transfer.

When a computer becomes obsolete, one does not discard the data it contains. The hardware is merely a temporary vehicle of implementation for structures of information. The data gets transferred to new systems for continued use. Decreasing costs of computer storage means that no information generated today ever need be lost.

We can consider building an artificial computational substrate both functionally and structurally identical to the brain (and perhaps the body). How? Via the predicted future capabilities of nanotechnology.[15]

Communicating nano-machines which pervade the organism may analyze the neural and cellular structure and transfer the information obtained to machinery capable of growing, atom by atom, an identical copy.

But what of the soul? According to the *American Heritage Dictionary*: "soul (is) the animating and vital principle in man credited with the faculties of thought, action and emotion and conceived as forming an immaterial entity distinguishable from but temporarily coexistent with his body."

At first reading this definition seems to be a classic example of theological nonsense. But studied from the perspective of information theory we may be able to wrestle this religio-babble into scientific operations. Let's change the bizarre word "immaterial" to "invisible to the naked senses," i.e., atomic/molecular/electronic. Now the "soul" refers to information processed and stored in microscopic-cellular, molecular packages. Soul becomes any information that "lives," i.e., is capable of being retrieved and communicated. Is it not true that all the tests for "death" at every level of measurement (nuclear, neural, bodily, galactic) involve checking for unresponsiveness to signals?

From this viewpoint, the twenty-two immortality options become cybernetic methods of preserving one's unique signal capacity. There are as many souls as there are ways storing and communicating data. Tribal lore defines the racial soul. DNA is a molecular soul. The brain is a neurological soul. Electron storage creates the silicon soul. Nanotechnology makes possible the atomic soul.

22. Computer Viral: Persistent Existence in Gibson's Cyberspace Matrix.

The previous option permitted personal survival through isomorphic mapping of neural structure to silicon (or some

[15] We partially regret such speculations beyond present technical capabilities. The brain is a most complex machine, with some 10^{20} individual cells. Yet we are redeemed by what we see as the technical inevitability of nanotechnology.

other arbitrary medium of implementation). It also suggests the possibility of survival as an entity in what amounts to a reification of Jung's collective unconscious: the global information network.

In the 21st century imagined by William Gibson, wily cybernauts will not only store themselves electronically, but do so in the form of a "computer virus," capable of traversing computer networks and of self-replication as a guard against accidental or malicious erasure by others, or other programs. (Imagine the somewhat droll scenario: "What's on this CD?" "Ah, that's just old Leary. Let's go ahead and reformat it.")

Given the ease of copying computer-stored information, one could exist simultaneously in many forms. Where the "I" is in this situation is a matter for philosophy. Our belief is that consciousness would persist in each form, running independently (and ignorant of each other self-manifestation unless in communication with it), cloned at each branch point.

NOTE

These options for Voluntary-Reversible-Metabolic Coma and auto-metamorphosis are not mutually exclusive. The intelligent person needs little encouragement to explore all of these possibilities, and to design new other alternatives to going belly-up in line with Management Memos.

Kon-Tiki of the Flesh

In the near future, what is now taken for granted as the perishable human creature will be a mere historical curiosity, one point amidst unimaginable multidimensional diversity of form. Individuals, or groups of adventurers, will be free to choose to reassume flesh-and-blood form, constructed for the occasion by the appropriate science.

Such historical expeditions may well be conducted in the spirit of Thor Heyerdahl's Kon Tiki voyages. To voyage in what the light of history reveals to be an objectively improbable way, merely to prove that such was possible, as unlikely as it seems.

THUS SPOKE THE POPE

by Pope Nick the One

A woman lies in a hospital bed, just minutes from death. She can barely move her wasting, crippled, pain-wracked body, but her mind is still sharp.

As she treasures the irretrievable years of her life, she is ready, even eager to experience her death: "I don't want to live like this," she says to herself and to anyone who will listen. Many times in these last days she has asked for help to end her life. But the doctors and nurses and orderlies all refuse. "It would not be moral, or legal, or ethical or proper," they say.

Suddenly, we hear from a television set:

"News Flash. We interrupt this program to bring you the following important news bulletin. Universal Biologicals announced today the creation of an almost unbelievable new process which they call FY^1. The company says that the process provides an almost instantaneous rejuvenation of all cellular material by determining the original DNA pattern for each cell and then restoring the cells to perfect health. In other words, this new process is *The Fountain of Youth*. For more, here is Dr. Timothy Leary, the President of Universal Biologicals:

'People of the Planet Earth. If this stuff does what we think it does, No One Has To Die Anymore. Though extensive testing has been done on FY^1, we realize that there is still much more to do before we can feel confident that this new process is truly safe. We don't want to distribute something which we believe will extend everyone's life and later find out it's dangerous. At the same time, there are people out there right now whose life might be saved by this process. So, we have decided to make FY[1] available immediately to anyone near death who wants it. Shipments are arriving at hospitals everywhere at this very moment. To those of you who are healthy, I say, wait until we get more information about this process. If you become terminally ill during our testing cycle, you can choose to take FY[1] or not at that time. And if you are dying now, you can have FY[1] within minutes, if you want it.' "

The woman is overwhelmed. "Did I hear that right? Am I hallucinating in my last moments?" She gathers her last bit of strength and reaches for the button to call the nurse. It is the last minute reprieve from death she never imagined she might have. "Nurse," she calls, "did you hear that. I can be young and vital and alive again. I don't have to suffer this agonizing death. I want you to get me some of that stuff right away."

"Yes, I heard that evil man," the nurse says. "Immortality indeed! It's the work of the devil. There is only one path to immortality. Here at Blessed Mary's Hospital of Holy Suffering none of us will have anything to do with this evil and you won't either. Be content, Ma'am, a priest is on the way; you'll be with Jesus soon."

Fade to black.

For me this is Horror. Like Winston Smith and rats. Like the soldier who imagines the last bullet coming straight for his head at the moment of the armistice, I fear that I will be the last mortal on this planet. And I am ENRAGED at the thought of this.

**WE ARE THE FIRST OF THE IMMORTALS,
OR THE LAST OF THE MORTALS
AND THE ONLY THING STANDING BETWEEN
THEM IS STUPIDITY.**

For me, the "problems" of immortality come down to only two issues: the technology to accomplish the extension of life, and the decision of each individual to use, or not use, the technology as it becomes available. For the first time in the history of this planet, so far as we know, the probability of significant life extension is upon us. It is likely that within the next very few years human lifetimes above 100–150 active, productive years will be practical. To me, that means that you who are reading these words now have a high likelihood of living for as long as you want, for if you can live for another hundred or so years, during that time the bio-technology will continue to advance so that you can live for 200, 300, 500 or more years and in the ensuing time more research, more advances and a longer lifetime. Functional Physical Immortality.

So, for me, the issue is simple and leads to many exciting questions. How will the human species be changed by the prospect of a longer life? What will man become as some leave the planet and travel through the solar system and then to the stars? What new species will man create from himself to deal with new environments, new challenges? How will the human race deal with the issue of *meaning* in a lifetime beyond breeding, rearing and death?

To me, *these* are the kinds of issues that are important for the future of mankind. The technology is coming, some humans are "ready" for it, even more eagerly await it.

But for many people on this planet, the issue evokes a myriad of other "problems." It is hard for me to keep from going off the deep end when I hear alleged human beings utter questions like: Should we *allow* life extension technology to be developed? If it is, who should be *allowed* to have it? If we allow the technology to be used, *what will happen* to an already over-crowded planet?

And some people raise even more wacko pseudo-issues: Is the pursuit of immortality *moral*? (This kind of question really uncovers their game. This is the came crap-trap of words that kept millions of people in misery and poverty in the middle ages—i.e., up to today, because suffering and death is "God's will," or "karma," or "fate" or "natural.") Or, what does [fill in name of your favorite god] say about immortality? (Personally, I don't give a flying fuck.) Or, how can man achieve salvation if he doesn't die? (As a child were you subjected to such obscenities as "If I die before I wake" and "Cross my heart and hope to die"?) Or, how about this one: why should anyone care about his own physical death when the species (or the state, or the collective unconscious) will go on? (Well, marvelous one, I don't care about those things since *I* won't be here. Oh, sure, my *molecules* will be around feeding some worm, but as far as I know, the *I* won't be.) Or, (and this is the one that really sets me off): since I'm sure that I have an immortal soul, *you* shouldn't be concerned about extending *your* life. (If there is some sort of life after death, that's great, a bonus. And if you are convinced, go ahead and die; after all, the real issue here is *choice*. However, since I have no convincing data that such theories are based on anything real, how about we investigate these things in the leisure of a limitless life?)

When I hear these insanities, I know what it must be like for an eagle, used to roaming the skies at will, to be caught in a net and destined to a life of misery in a cage six by six by six...

And now you see why I have so much trouble with the issue of immortality. For me the whole thing seems so simple: when will the technology be available. And that leads me to feelings of joyous anticipation and *hope*. But for so many people the issue has nothing to do with longer life but is one of *who owns whom*. And when I realize that, I feel murderously angry.

Take another look at the "questions" about life-extension and ask yourself what they imply about an individual's ownership of his/her own life. Read any newspaper on any day and you may be overwhelmed to find how much implies (but usually does not deal with) the issue of ownership of human beings: What should "we" do about the homeless? Sexual abuse? Illegal aliens? What should "government funds" (taxes) be spent for? How can "we" win the "war" on drugs? How can we save the resources of the planet, especially the most precious resource, "our" children? How can we accommodate the olde Roman Catholic Church's dogma about surrogate mothers, the American Medical Association's hatred of "quackeries" (i.e., competitors), how do "we" manage the impact of computers, space exploration, land use, etc. etc. etc.

Who is the "we" in all these questions? And where do "you" fit in? The answer: you will either be in compliance, in a jail, in a mental institution, or in a box.

So the issue of immortality, as almost all issues on this wretched, backward planet, has been made into one of power. As always that threatens your life and mine. Literally. What resources would it take to develop life extension technology? How much time, how much money, how much will? Instead those resources are expended on wars on drugs, wars on ideologies, witch hunts and man hunts. We are traveling on a circular track, going around and around, never noticing that the terrain never changes.

How can you expect a culture which forbids you any choice about your own *death* to have any respect for your *life*? How can we expect societies which hate men for being alive to care about extending that life? "The world is wonderful, it's only human beings that make it miserable." Man as alien to this planet.

Original sin. The evil of the ego.

Ah, yes, the ego. The twentieth century mark of the beast. The thing to be killed in man. Always there is something to be killed in man. What is it about the ego that is so dangerous? Why is concern for your own life the brand of immaturity, insensitivity and evil? Why are all of Jung's archetypes, even the Shadow, so accepted, but not the archetype of the Ego?

I encourage you to take part in the destruction of man's greatest and only enemies, death & stupidity. Find the cure for death; if you can't do that, support those who can. And through it all, resist those who would enslave your life.

The New Man
is no longer waiting
in the wings.
She is waiting in your head

BREAKING OUT

Those of us who still have a breath of real life in us, who refuse to close the "doors of perception" on command have concluded that:

WE . . . . . ARE . . . . . ON . . . . . STRIKE

We DEMAND that the world place its resources at the door of research to END DEATH and STUPIDITY.

Dr. Hyatt says:

SHAKE OFF THE AMNESIA

There are only two enemies
which all WoMen of planet earth share:

DEATH & STUPIDITY

How can a whole Planet
Get H—Y—P—N—O—T—I—Z—E—D into
believing that
DEATH IS INEVITABLE?

How can we continue on our daily routine, when IMMORTALITY is staring us in the face? How can we think about anything more important

than our own lives
and the lives of those we love?

How can we accept this
RUTHLESS MANIPULATION?

Why do we still buy these
US–EL–ESS theories of heaven, hell,
reincarnation, karma?
What good are these placebofors
when—within striking distance—
is the real thing?

the

ICE-CREAM

"IN-itself."

Don't depend on anyone else to do it for you.

DO IT YOURSELF . . .. NOW!

Forget the image, the new shoes for the decaying feet, the new car. Put your MONEY WHERE YOUR LIFE IS.

Join me and others, create a FUND, not for your retirement but for your eternal FUTURE. Become a participant in IMMORTALITY

NOW!

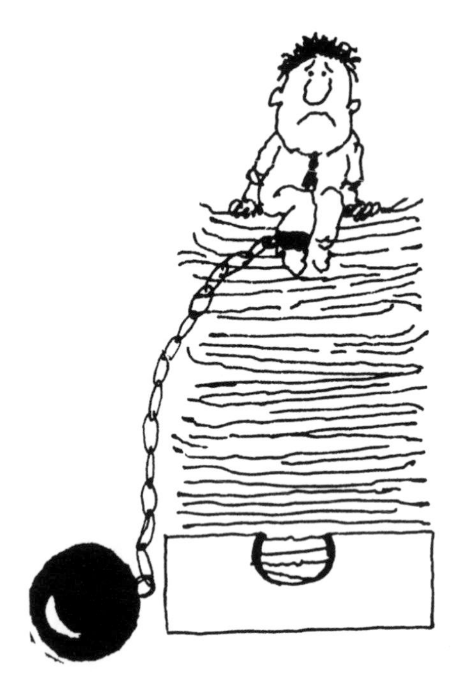

BREAK TRANCE—NOW IF YOU CHOOSE

THE PROBLEM WITH THE WORLD IS...

THE PROBLEM WITH THE WORLD IS . . .
"As long as they believe that stuff, we're sure to win!!
STUPIDITY
DEATH
"POOR EDUCATION"
"RACISM"
"DRUGS"
"GOVERNMENTS"
"TOXIC WASTE"
"COMMUNISM"
"THE BANKING SYSTEM"
"QUEERS"
"THE YOUNGER GENERATION"
"GERM WARFARE"

PETITION

THE PROBLEM WITH THE WORLD IS . . .

"As long as they believe that stuff, we're sure to win!!

"POOR EDUCATION"
"RACISM"
"DRUGS"
"GOVERNMENTS"
"TOXIC WASTE"
"COMMUNISM"
"THE BANKING SYSTEM"
"QUEERS"
"THE YOUNGER GENERATION"
"GERM WARFARE"

STUPIDITY
DEATH

Sign this petition and send it to your legislator!

OWNERSHIP OF HUMANS

STRICTLY

PROHIBITED

one by one

by Jim Goldiner

one by one
or in any
combination

like a starched
beehive the
enemy
camps in the
enemy's camp

one bleating
stone hearing
its own echo
, they, like the
STUKA
make festering
sores of affections

too much to
see that like
some insipid
substance
their iniquity
clings to their
own avalanche
until
they're before
their own fall
looking up from
some helpless pit

that is not
to say innocuous
but dead!

WHO OWNS THE PLANET EARTH?

Good and Evil—As Primitive "Natural Law"

by Christopher S. Hyatt, Ph.D.

The Scene: The Space Ship Enterprise.

The Question: Kirk to Spock—Who owns the Planet Earth and its inhabitants?

The Answer: Spock to Crew—Those who have the power to define. Those who have the power to lie well.

The ownership of the Planet has changed hands a hundred times. I think if you trace their papers back far enough one of their first owners was called Jehovah. Approximately 18% of the present population still believe He and His Son still own the planet and they have been chosen to rule the rest.

The earthlings have an interesting habit of dividing up ownership through wars and then marking their territory on little scraps of paper. The inhabitants of each territory think they are superior to their neighbors. This in turn creates new wars and new divisions. This is their particular form of making changes. It is difficult for them to change without being forced to or having some horrible event take place.

They use primitive genetic practices. Conquered regions are used as experimental breeding grounds. When they ran out of new frontiers and artificially attempted to stabilize the planet there were four main classes of people. The intelligent and powerful, the status quo, the poor and the criminal. When they invented space travel the powerful and the criminals left, the poor were slaughtered and the ownership of the planet passed to the Status Quo. These were known as the middle class of mid-zonal professionals who from their inception have attempted to imitate the powerful and intelligent. They in turn re-invented the same four classes and the ownership of the planet is up for grabs. The majority of the problems on this planet are the result of the idea that humans are not sovereign and autonomous, but property owned by primitive Gods and incompetent governments. At this time the United States believes it is the most competent and elite.

It is important to remember when visiting this planet that words, things and thinking are experienced by the inhabitants as the same. They are full of pride, easily hurt and capable of just about anything. They suffer from a poor memory when it comes to self improvement and an excellent one when it comes to remembering slights and imagined injuries.

They enjoy the game known as scapegoat. This is a game where they find someone less powerful to blame their problems on. Often they will torture, enslave and murder their victims. As I said and it warrants repeating, the inhabitants respond to words and pictures with the same neuro-physiological reactions as real events. Be cautious, it can get quite dangerous down there. They are very aware of differences and at times respond with curiosity but tend to respond with violence.

SCENE TWO

The Dawning of popular Western Metaphysics (or The History of Metaphor) is best expressed by the story of the Tree of Knowledge, when an imagined, undifferentiated, blissful world called the Garden of Eden was suddenly split apart when a female member of the species ate an apple and then tempted her mate to do the same. Adam and Eve's act of disobedience, born from a womb of curiosity, divided the world into two. Good and evil became primary modes of thinking and reacting and members of the species have proceeded to develop entire philosophies from this metaphor. As I have said, although very childish, they are also very inventive.

The primal set of concepts, **good and evil,** springs from *disobedience,* the very well spring of God's greatest gift, man's free will. It was the very use of this gift which inescapably gave birth to shame, guilt, original sin and planetary bankruptcy. It seems that intention transforms accidents into crimes.

Expelled from paradise into a world of gravity and work mankind must now forever struggle for his act of primal disobedience.

From an idyllic world free from pain, man found himself in the world of change, of differences and similarities, of epistemology, and of language, a tool which can cut in two directions at the same time. The ancient Hawaiian's have a proverb which says, "In language is life and death."

From the simple myth of Eden which almost every Western child is familiar, sprang a world view, which, in its extreme, is represented by modern day earth television evangelism. It appears, that God is a landlord, indeed a slumlord, but always a Lord. Man is an ungrateful, rebellious slave-child who can never pay his debt, except possibly by complete obedience, casting his mind and nature into the "caring" hands of his angry and frustrated Creator.

SCENE THREE

This species' philosophy has enjoyed centuries of speculating on the fruits of this primal disobedience—The emergence of the Opposites. Some of these opposites have been Nature/Nurture, Being/Becoming, Whole/Part, Real/Apparent, Mind/Body, Physical/Spiritual, Man/God and other meta-morsels.

Any intelligent human could simply re-create the entire history of the planet by plotting the Opposites, both as independent grids and or as interactive forces over time. In fact we could diagnose or mirror an individual or an entire culture's development simply by understanding which position on each grid a group's belief system is plotted. For example, the Chinese believe in fate, the Americans believe in free will.

It Is Amazing How Something Can Evolve From Nothing

"Opposites" (either/ors) have served as epistemological training ground for metaphysicians who could demonstrate their superiority to the masses by turning an apple into an orange. Of course, only those divinely ordained to understand the true meaning of these terms could participate in this sport. The rest stood in awe and worshipped those who had the credentials and ability to understand the dark and mysterious world(s) of Being and Becoming.

The problem of opposites lies in the inadequate information gained from the Tree of Knowledge—good and evil. When man learned about good and evil he did not learn how words are like containers that can be filled with just about any type of liquid.

Like a child who receives an airplane for a gift and is so delighted and overwhelmed by the way the wheels turn, he never learns that the plane, if used differently, can fly. The utter emptiness of words gave man the opportunity to fill them with whatever he needed, while at the same time believing the words had an independent substance of their very own.

The opposites have served as a primitive model of classifying, ordering and understanding the universe. Their real use is the their speed and ease allowing for quick reactions in dangerous situations. The grunt "UGH" means run.

Although the species has changed from its beginnings it still prefers to rely on opposites rather than even simple interacting grids.

In other words, the notion of opposites is not a "natural law," but simply a primitive survival device with many interesting and dangerous uses. If we carefully examine history we will find that man has torn himself apart with his belief in the REALITY and NECESSITY of Either/Ors.

For the man in the street, the philosophies of opposites, particularly Good and Evil, have served as a torture chamber, a crucifix made from metaphor. Thrust into a world which views him as the property of Gods and States and overwhelmed by an unrepayable debt, the metaphysics of slavery and the facts of pain, pleasure and death; bolstered by science, whose theorists have become the whores of the state, man is now informed that he is ill. The proof of this is his refusal to submit completely. The world debt is due to his saying "no" to total slavery. He will not obey. We are at War, and man is the enemy. The question is: Who is on the other side?

Original sin is now *also* translated into sickness, calling in a new and scientific priest craft who rush to the rescue. Man is sick, addicted, lame, and dangerous, needing constant protection and supervision by the state, insurance companies, and a never-ending parade of caring, licensed professionals. We are told over and over again that man's illness and addictions are costing *US* billions. Man the slave/resource, is causing *US* trouble, he is interfering with *OUR* Plans. Man's debt has now increased a billion-fold. Those who question the "plans" or the sanity of the metaphors in play, are diagnosed as morally unfit or mentally ill.

SCENE FOUR

Evil emerges as a metaphor which refers to those who refuse to accept the Plan—the prevailing Garden of Eden—created by God so She may bestow Her Love and Grace. If man refuses he must be force-fed.

What makes the notion of Evil and Good work is the belief that the words have substance independent of the workings of man's own mind and his uncanny need and ability to create *final causes.*

All that is required for metaphysics to function, to perform its magic, is any unanswered question which can be associated with fear and pain. What makes a leader is someone who claims that he can fill the void.

THE NEXT SCENE

While most humans agree that slavery is evil—that the ownership of one human by another is immoral—few humans equate slavery with enforced education, welfare, health, and the idea of a perfect orderly universe. Slavery is usually associated with power over others and with the ability to enforce one's will on another without the fear of retaliation. Within the "right" of ownership and debt there is a hidden mystery—a metaphysics—a knowledge only available to those with the power to create and enforce their metaphysics. Whenever a new group achieves power, they also inherit the metaphysics, and magically, the ability to use it.

However, an interesting twist has taken place in the entire slave/master paradigm. Enforced education, welfare, health, *are for our own good and it is our duty to submit to the treatment.* This is immediately followed by the platitude *that all these laws are necessary for the smooth functioning of society, which, of course, we all observe daily. Without someone to run the show we would have chaos and disorder.* This is followed by a SMILE, and the statement that "things could be worse."

Modern slavery is not simply a "Thou Shalt Not," but numerous "Thou Shalts." Many liberated humans even believe that it is the obligation of the Masters to care for their Slaves. Of course, what is different is the title-word "citizen" and that today's *sophisticated* redistribution of power *shows* no blood during family hour TV.

We can begin to scent the meaning of evil. It smells of change, contradiction, uncertainties. It is the *lack of* stability, becoming, the *opposite of* order, being, peace, the good. Here the confusion coincides with physiology. We have mixed the whole thing up. We have confused the physiology of comfort, the cognition of stability, beliefs as truth, predictable futures, statistics—with the *idea* of a Morality. In other words, while chaos, disorder, change and destruction are integral and necessary elements of life on this heavy G planet, we abhor its realization and worse yet, its *Existence.* This requires the postulation of its opposite as an Ideal a heaven juxtaposed against earth. A God who loathes his Creation. From this has evolved a need to group act, to over-control and "normalize." We are simply No-Good Shits—by Definition.

From this we have created the Idea of the one God, separated from his creation by Evil. The new slavery, unlike the old, not only *guarantees* that the slave will be punished if he transgresses, but also *guarantees* stability, order, health and education—by decree. The new slave must let God (State) bestow care and supervision onto her, in order to ensure the continuing "safe" functioning of the person as resource. If the person refuses, denies the right of the Master and his Plan, the person is Evil. It is important to remember (the story of Job stresses this), Evil cannot be a characteristic of the Master, only the Slave. When the slave gets smart she reverses the process.

Mind and Will are exchanged for a *guaranteed* future. But even a modern slave cannot tolerate the complete awareness of the exchange. Acknowledging his cowardice and slave mentality would offend his "pride." To cover up the trade, we require more fictions and ideologies.

We now search for the enemy of stability, as if it had a face, an identity, other than life itself.

And our search for those who cause the discomfort is directed at the rebels. Those who dare rattle the cage of stability.

The rebel the one who sought and tamed new frontiers, once revered as hero and mystic, is now turned into the sociopath. This transformation from hero to devil is partially a result of the stability demanded by those who come after him (the middle class) to live off the fruits of his courage and struggle, the mass which comes to fill the world carved by those who thrived on nature's unpredictable chaotic qualities. Once the frontier is "tamed" Status Quo moves in and demands order. A place where they can build their nests and ensure the betterment of their genetic coils. Morality is in fact an invention for the Middle Class. It creates a notion of order and justice in the world. The truly Powerful do not require these fictions and the Poor…well, they know better.

What of the rebel now? If lucky, he became wealthy and powerful, and with that, mobile, able to keep out of reach of those who require tranquillity and predictability in order to breed. If unlucky, he is forcibly exiled, jailed or murdered.

However, this is not the end of the story, for Nature "knows" that it cannot survive without the rebel. She is born again and again, and when born into stability, taming is difficult. The child is incorrigible, delinquent, hyperactive, requiring Ritalin, psychotherapy, special education. If lucky, the child escapes with the deep scars of guilt, shame and self-hatred, but at least having a chance to find its own frontier. If unlucky, the child is tortured, jailed, or suffers from never-ending despair.

When there is no frontier for the rebel the soul of a society begins to suffer. Some, like Wilhelm Reich, contend that the culture can itself be diseased. He referred to this as the Emotional Plague. In the end he was proven correct, not simply by the culture, but by individuals who embodied the repressed counterparts of an ideal.

According to Jungian tradition the manifestation or experience of evil results from the repression of both the personal and the collective **shadow,** sometimes resulting in physical manifestations such as Hitler, regarded in this age as the Epitome of Evil. However, what is the cause of this repression but the Ideal itself? In the face of this intimation, why still worship the Ideal?

As Nietzsche so beautifully put it, the ideal of truth posited by the Christian world, was the value which overturned it. Can we say that our *fear and denial* of instability or disorder, which in my view is the result of a lack of belief in ourselves as anything but a slave race, be perceived as more devastating than chaos and instability itself? The attempt to destroy evil, in and of itself, is an attempt to destroy life. Accepting that disobedience was the first evil, it follows that any attempt to destroy disobedience is an attempt to destroy life. I believe that even the rebel Jesus would agree that his acts of dis-obedience were perceived as evil by the establishment Rabbis, who used the notion of evil to destroy him.

To understand what a "civilized Christian society" means by Evil, we should dilate on Hitler's aspirations. He saw himself on a Messianic mission to purify and help his definition of perfected man evolve and rule the world. He saw himself and his followers as the Masters and the rest of the world as slaves. He was willing to do anything to see his vision fulfilled, including Usurping the Power of Mass Murder from God (see the Flood). But remember Usurping is the greater sin.

He performed his willful acts openly and told the world what his intentions were. He brought to consciousness a picture of mass evil (something which everyone else was doing, but behind more-or-less closed doors). Was his Sin any different when compared to Stalin, Mao, Genghis Khan, the Christian and Islamic inquisitions, and the hundreds of other cultures, civilizations and religions which have thought of themselves as Chosen, on a Mission, superior and willing to murder for the Ideal? Could we say then, that his evil was simply losing, or was it the "more important" fact that he employed violence? If so, what of the American Indian, and other races and cultures destroyed by the Christian notion of a pure white race. And what of the Blacks in America? No, most humans would argue that Hitler's evil was something more. What was it? It may have been because it happened in our own time, it was blatant, he lost the war, he crossed his genetic borders, or attacked the "chosen people" or ??

(As an aside, I would like to inform the reader that some individuals, after reading this, have asked me if I was a National Socialist simply because I used Hitler as an example!)

The word Evil functions in such a way as to allow one group to justify its own atrocities and make them noble. By dealing with such a powerful metaphysical abstraction (one which is physiologically associated with pain, fear, trembling and survival), it is an easy step to the performance of an act such as "execution," with the sense of moral righteousness and vindication. It is not a man who is being executed, it is Evil. It is the void filled with all the imagination and terror of a cowardly "adjusted" Status Quo man.

What is the psychological effect on the slave of the following two statements?

1) We will execute anyone who disobeys.
2) We will execute anyone who is evil.

As Nietzsche has shown, evil is an invention serving a purpose. It allows one group to justify its *will to power* over another, just as it has been used to intimidate most men.

REBELS AND DEVILS

The rebel with a cause is one who risks the label of evil when she attempts to remove—or go beyond—the categories of limitation currently believed. Just like the notion of the four-minute-mile which once became "eternally" defined as an Absolute, the rebel challenges arbitrary definitions, commandments and rules, which are believed to be Absolute. Some of these are death, gravity, limitations of the body and intelligence.

What we do and how we feel is a function of believing in fictitious limitations which have no basis except in habits.

Good and Evil and Opposites in general are primitive devices used by our minds to order the universe, and in my view, create an atmosphere of conflict which might not otherwise exist. The meaning and truth ascribed to the various pairs of opposites including such famous arguments as Nature/Nurture are a function of Who has the Power to create Definitions and, thereby, Offenders.

If the human mind requires "evil" in order to function, let it be death, stupidity, gravity and disease. If the human mind requires the notion of "good," let it be ceasing the primitive process of projecting our Greatness onto Idols—accepting Evil onto Ourselves.

WHO OWNS YOU?

The following table shows three models of OWNERSHIP: The first is the Model of God; the second, derived from the first, is the Model of Society and its Caretakers. The third is the Model of the Cyber-Shaman (aka the Rebel-Devil).

OWNERSHIP TABLE:
WHO OWNS WHOM?

MODEL ONE: GOD	MODEL TWO: SOCIETY & ITS CARETAKERS	MODEL THREE: THE REBEL-DEVIL
God OWNS Man	Society OWNS Man	Man OWNS Hirself
God is the Center and Perfect	Society is the Center and Perfect	Life is the Center
Man is Sinful	Man is Sick	Man is ?
Religion	Law	Philosophy
Priest	Politician/Doctor	Cyber-Philosopher/ Adventurer
Sin/Pathology	Pathology & Rebelliousness	Functionality & Good Will
God is Studied	Man is Studied as a problem	Life is Studied as an interest
One Up/ One Down	One Up/ One Down	Shifting Systems of Probabilistic Truth
Oppression	Oppression	Essential Cooperation
Adaptation to God's Will	Adaptation to Society's Will	Grow to Possibilities of Self

One purpose of this OWNERSHIP TABLE is to help the individual gain insight into fundamentalist attitudes of Ownership.

Only when man OWNS HIRSELF is the dehumanizing process of slavery non-existent. The notion of OWNERSHIP, be it explicit or tacit, is the KEY CONCEPT which determines what is thought of as a problem and what solutions can be offered.

If we accept the Model of the Cyber-Shaman (that man OWNS HIRSELF), 95 percent of the so-called problems—which we read about in newspapers, hear about on the radio, watch on television, and discuss with friends—*Do Not Exist.* Thus, all proposed *Solutions* for these *Pseudo-Problems* are *Meaningless.*

The concept of OWNERSHIP starts in the cradle and does not end—not even in the grave.

Thus, our solution is not the eradication of

OWNERSHIP

but rather

REPOSSESSING the SELF

Frranzzz!

by Jim Goldiner

Frranzzz!
Frranzzz Kaaafka!
can you hear me Franz
or have they really done you in for good

my time has come round again

i lost the case on the first trial
no appeal allowed of course
this i understood
but they let me go

And Franz ive done it again
i got myself into the same fix
and i love it Franz
i love it

Only one question
will i get the same judge and jury

Why Is It?

by Jim Goldiner

Why is it
that after devouring the fruit of a ripe olive
and being confronted with just the pit
and not knowing what it really is
and therefore what to do with it,
we toss it to the wind

Rear Admiral Hyatt fighting the War Against Stupidity

As Tim says: *Be Polite!* "Just say No THANK You to Death & Stupidity"

ZINGOTS & EARTHLINGS

Notes to those who
— Live in Opposites —
No-one except a Spiritualist
knows
what
— Matter —
is.

Hyatt will now undertake
the dirty job of
CHANGING THE NAME
of
THE PLANET

— Preying to Dirt —
a species identifying itself with
dirt and clay is bad for our
Self-Esteem

It is time for us to become

Zingots and not Dirtlings

Within 30 years physicists will discover
Zingatrons
as the fundamental basis of the universe

AND

IT IS NOT CLAY!

With this: What we call

Psyche & Matter

will become Empty Notions—

Plato & Aristotle will politely
disappear

into

the

Zingatron

If you PLEASE
WAKE-UP
NOW!

Time to Think
Clearly
about
What To Do.

If you can
sleep you can
WAKE UP

Further Trances
— Sense & Feel —
A Modern Shaman's Guide
to
A
Pregnant Universe

by
Hyatt & Antero Alli